GETTING INTO COMPUTERS

Chapter 2 is on Computer Language or Terminology

GETTING INTO COMPUTERS

A CAREER GUIDE TO TODAY'S HOTTEST NEW FIELD

IRV BRECHNER

BALLANTINE BOOKS • NEW YORK

Copyright © 1983 by Irv Brechner

All rights reserved under International and Pan-American Copyright Conventions. Published in the United States by Ballantine Books, a division of Random House, Inc., New York, and simultaneously in Canada by Random House of Canada Limited, Toronto.

Library of Congress Catalog Card Number: 82-90838

ISBN 0-345-30172-2

Cover design: Tony Russo
Cover photo: David Spindell

Manufactured in the United States of America

First Edition: June 1983

10 9 8 7 6 5 4 3 2 1

Dedicated to
Kathi, for inspiration and perspiration
Jay, for information and organization
Alan, for getting me started, and
Howard, Frances, Stanley, Larry, Nancy, Claire and Fred . . .
for being there to share.

CONTENTS

INTRODUCTION GETTING STARTED IN COMPUTING ... ix

PART I LOOKING AT THE WHOLE PICTURE ... 1
1. The Computer Age: What It's All About ... 3
2. A Basic Primer ... Nothing Technical ... 11
3. Looking Ahead: Computer Applications Today ... and in the Future ... 16
4. The Employment Scene ... 26

PART II CAREERS WITHIN THE COMPUTER INDUSTRY: JOB DESCRIPTIONS ... 33
5. The Four Career Areas ... 35
6. Design and Manufacturing ... 38
7. Service, Maintenance, and Installation ... 72
8. Word and Data Processing ... 76
9. Sales, Marketing, and Retailing ... 95

PART III AN INSIDE LOOK AT OTHER CAREERS USING COMPUTERS ... 103
10. End-Users: A Special Group Offering Special Careers ... 105
11. Careers in Twelve Different Work Areas ... 108

PART IV EDUCATION AND PREPARATION ... 129
12. Education ... 131
13. Job Hunting and Recruiting ... 144
14. Windup ... 155

PART V RESOURCES ... 157
15. Publications ... 159
16. Organizations ... 182

INTRODUCTION
GETTING STARTED
IN COMPUTING

Computer people have many favorite expressions, two of them being "hands on" and "getting started." They're friendly ways of saying "let's get ready, sit down at a keyboard, and begin computing."

Before we begin analyzing, planning, and discussing a potential career in computing, let's loosen up, put careers out of our minds for a minute and pretend we're sitting in front of a computer. It doesn't matter what kind—a small personal microcomputer or a large mainframe that fills up an entire room. Picture the computer as friendly, inviting you to use it as a productive and meaningful tool.

The first thing you'll notice about our imaginary computer is that it's made up of three major components. The central processing unit (CPU) is the heart of the computer, responsible for its performance. It is "the computer." The keyboard is what you type on in order to get information into the computer; and the tape drive or disk drive is used for storage of information. We'll get into how computers work and the buzzwords associated with them later, but for now let's assume your computer is turned on, ready to go.

What you'll notice next about our computer is the speed at which it can process or complete a transaction or problem. Let's take an example.

Suppose I were a potential employer offering you a job at a certain salary, and that you came back to me and said, "I'll work for one penny on the first day if you will double my salary for a month. That would be two cents the second day, four cents the third, and so forth. I'll take whatever the result is instead of your offer."

If you multiply this out, you'll see that what we're talking about is millions of dollars. If you have a calculator, see how much time it takes you to figure this out. With practice, it took me forty-five seconds; perhaps you could do better. However, within two weeks after purchasing a personal computer, I was able to write a short five-line program which solved this problem in under two seconds!

Computer speed is what accounts for the dramatic problem-solving efficiency we hear so much about. And miniaturization makes this awesome power and speed possible at almost inconceivably small sizes. In 1960, the typical processor had 100 active components (electrical parts) per cubic centimeter (CCM). Today the figure is 10 million components/CCM, and by 1990 the prediction is another 1,000 times that!

Let's look at this from another angle. One dollar could buy the execution (processing) of 100,000 single operations (like adding or subtracting) in the late 1950s. In the 1960s the figure was 1 million operations per dollar, and by 1970, more than 100 times greater than that! Computer capacity that cost $30,000 in 1970 cost just $4,000 in 1977, and could cost less than $100 within two to three years from now!

The rate of growth of computer companies also offers some spectacular numbers. The overall field is expected to grow well over 100 percent annually in the next decade, compared to projected growth rates of 19 to 28 percent in other top-notch fields. Individual firms already established in the field have growth records which are astronomical. *INC* magazine, a publication aimed at smaller corporations, puts out a "Top 100" list similar to the *Fortune* 500. For the period 1976 to 1980, nine of the top fifteen firms were computer related.

The worst performing firm on this list (#100) had a growth rate of over 500 percent in those four years. Number one's rate was 366,567 percent, a figure totally beyond belief and comprehension!

These figures aren't here to impress you, although they probably have. Their purpose is simple: to illustrate graphically the dynamic nature of the computer industry.

But choosing a career path in computing demands much more than just selecting a job that sounds good or an area that's appealing. Learning the dynamics of the field, the educational requirements, and the future projections of the industry is equally important to your future career satisfaction. And since computing will encompass almost every area of society and work, your ability to make intelligent, informed choices is vital.

My goal in *Getting into Computers* is twofold: to outline a wide range of jobs within the computer industry, each with a full description and background; and, more importantly, to make you aware of the total picture, in order that you may be better able to choose a career that will be most meaningful and productive.

Any personnel recruiter will tell you that because of the terrific growth of the industry, the eighties and beyond are indeed the right time to be career planning and hunting in computing. Use *Getting into Computers* smartly: study, plan, and get yourself into the right spot at the right time!

PART I
LOOKING AT THE WHOLE PICTURE

1. THE COMPUTER AGE: WHAT IT'S ALL ABOUT

The Intelligent Society. The Computer Age. The Micro Millennium. The Information Society. The Third Wave.

By whatever name or label, the future, indeed, is now. We are entering the most dynamic, fascinating, and mind-boggling period in the history of the world, one that will bring incredible change and offer a multitude of career opportunities worldwide. For those alive today, a rare opportunity exists to participate in changing the course of society by being a part of a major international revolution without arms.

What's the cause of this revolution? The computer, no longer a mysterious machine with blinking lights operated by a select few. From personal portables to monstrous mainframes, the computer is having the greatest impact on society of any machine ever invented, making the discovery of the wheel or the invention of the printing press pale by comparison. And what's more amazing yet is that the heart of the computer, the mighty computer chip, is no more than a tiny, razor-thin silicon wafer. Smaller than a fingernail and continually getting smaller, this speck of creation contains thousands of electrical circuits and can store more information than can be remembered by millions of people. Faster than a speeding bullet, it's also more accurate than all the world's scholars and has more energy than all the world's strongest men.

The computer is destined to play a part in all of our lives, both in every form of work and in all of our homes. Although just a few years ago only large firms could afford computers, today personal computers are being purchased and used with great success by individuals; within a decade, personal computers will be as commonplace as the home telephone, and will be the focal point of many of our daily activities: news, travel schedules, and special interactive television programming, just to name a few.

For computer companies, this growth represents an unimaginable windfall, and in fact new companies spring up almost daily. One of the rags-to-riches stories is that of Apple Computer.

Built in a garage with $1,500 worth of parts by two college dropouts, aged twenty-one and twenty-six, who hocked a van and calculator to get the money, the Apple personal computer has become the fairy tale of the industry. In four years, Apple has grown at an annual rate of over 43,000 percent, showing 1981 sales of over $334 million. They now employ over 2,400 people! But this is just one success story among hundreds, perhaps thousands.

Everyone, from hobbyists to big corporations, is cashing in. The number of computers produced in one year four years ago is now produced in one week!

Today's youth in school are learning with computers and are "computer literate," more so than much of the adult population. Teachers find that computer literacy is not hard to teach; it's easier, for instance, than teaching French to an American. Major educational publishers have set up computer software divisions to accompany their textbooks. Other firms have produced programs on basic living skills for school computers—everything from applying for credit to driver education. Sound incredible? It is!

The computer explosion is only in its infancy. But it is a baby that is worth $60 billion a year, a figure that should double within two years. And it will keep increasing at a phenomenal rate, with no real end in sight.

One of the major reasons for the incredible expansion of the computing industry is that computers are used in *all* fields. Everyone, from truckers to musicians, is either using computers now, or will be in the years to come. In fact, there is really no discipline exempt from the computer's incredible versatility. This explains why so many computers have been sold in such a short time, and why so many more will hit the market in the eighties.

The already strong impact that the computer has had, coupled with the tremendous growth forecast for it, will be responsible for shaping a whole new environment. But there will be a difficult transition period. People are now fearful of the computer, confused by it, and worried about loss of jobs and a world taken over by machines. They think computers are dehumanizing and impersonal. Yet once people get to know computers, they love them!

About the only potential negative factor in the whole picture is a possible decreased amount of social interaction, as people spend more time with machines than with other people. But unless you actually cut yourself off from others, there is plenty of "people power" in this business.

As for the question of job loss, a recent study by the U.S. Department of Labor indicates that the number of jobs lost to computers in the last thirty years has been more than offset by the number of jobs created as a result of computer efficiency. The field of clerical work, for instance, assumed by many to be a doomed career area, actually expanded from 10 million jobs in 1960 to 18 million in 1980—an 85 percent increase. No, there are no major job losses resulting from computerization that aren't offset by job increases.

What we have is a cloud with a fourteen-karat gold (not silver) lining. Computers, when combined with robots, will enable undesirable and dangerous production-line work to be handled without human interaction. This will result in better quality in some cases and a drastic decline in injuries and shortening of life spans due to on-the-job hazards. What we will also see are lowered costs on many products where computerization, both in design and actual manufacture, saves money or increases efficiency.

Those who are willing to recognize this phenomenon and change with the times will be rewarded with a career that's fulfilling, satisfying, and fun. The opportunities will be great for those who sense this and react favorably.

But for people who resist computers and lag behind, the situation will not look bright at all. Eventually ours will be a computer-based society. People who don't know the basics will be considered almost primitive.

Where does this all leave you, the person who has heard about computers and is thinking of getting into them? In the opinion of many, in great shape!

While our parents were happy to get almost any job to put bread on the table and clothes on their backs, the generation graduating in the eighties faces a different situation. Now it isn't good enough just to get a job. The situation is like a multiple-choice question in which all the answers are good. You must choose the best answer, just as you should secure the best career path based on your own personal traits and aspirations.

Fortunately, the fact that computers are compatible with almost any field makes the choice exciting. If your first love is medicine, you can combine medicine and computers. If you find retail selling interesting, retail computing might be for you. And if you want to be an accountant, you probably already know how helpful a computer can be. The choices are only limited by your imagination, since possibilities exist in every field where computers are used.

The whole scenario is mind boggling, not only to most of us but even to the people producing the computer equipment and software. Computers are a new phenomenon, and will be used by a new type of person who understands their depth and potential.

COMPUTERS AND SOCIETY

The future of society is reflected in the marketing of today's computers. Computers are no longer sold only to major corporations; many private individuals now own them as well. Some of the current advertising slogans aptly describe the goals of computer companies as well as the shift in our society. Vector Graphic uses the slogan "Computers for the advancement of society"; Honeywell uses "The ingenuity of people, the power of computers"; Digital uses "We change the way the world thinks"; and a host of others aiming their advertising at the general public use slogans such as Texas Instruments' "We put computing within everyone's reach," or Atari's "Computers for people." Not only is involvement with computing power by a huge segment of the population the goal of marketers, it is also the inevitable result of mankind's technological progress into the Information Age.

Two social issues which are now becoming important topics for discussion are computer literacy and the social impact of computing. Computer literacy—that is, whatever you need to know to function in an information-based society—is perhaps the most important phrase to come along in a long time. We all must accept computers as one of the most beneficial pieces of machinery ever developed. We, and especially our young people, must grow up with computers, learn about them and work with them so that their full benefits can be realized.

Adults cannot afford to discourage the use of computers by their children or grandchildren simply because they themselves haven't yet adapted. The youth of today must be open to the computer world of tomorrow, not suppressed by people who don't want to change.

Adults should learn to approach computers as kids do—by pounding away on the keys, experimenting, and having fun. Kids haven't received incorrect computer bills, so they approach computing without any bias. That's what adults should try to do as well.

THE INFORMATION AGE

Why do we call this the Information Age? Let's back up and take a quick look at history in order to gain perspective on the impact of computers on society—an important perspective to have when considering a career in computing.

There have been basically three major periods in the recent development of modern mankind. In the Agricultural Age most people worked outdoors growing and harvesting food. This work was done by hand or with primitive machines, and in this era, most of the goods produced and the monies made were agriculture-related.

The next major period was the Industrial Age, during which the development of machinery shifted the production emphasis from agriculture to the manufacturing of products by machines. Now man made all kinds of products, and the importance of agriculture in relation to the total economy declined. With this change in emphasis came an increased demand for jobs in the industrial sector and a decline in employment opportunities for agricultural workers.

We are now at the beginning of the Information Age (just one of many names for this era), and the emphasis is again shifting—rapidly and dramatically. Since the 1950s we have become a society in which a large segment of the population handles and processes information, as opposed to a product you can see or hold in your hand. Today, more Americans work solely with information than in manufacturing and agriculture combined! We've changed almost overnight from a society of "muscle power" to one of "mind power"—from a goods-producing society to a service society—and the process of change keeps accelerating. With the new popularity of personal computers and the general if tentative acceptance of computing by the public, the information era has started to mature—seemingly very suddenly to most people.

How will the computer change our society as we know it today? For one thing, it will alter population centers. In the agricultural and industrial ages, cities were founded near major waterways, highways, or other means of transportation. Computing has already begun to change this. Today, many corporate branches, connected by telephone lines and satellites to their computers in the main office, are relocating to the suburbs. A few people are already working from their home computer terminals, with video conferencing cutting down on the number of business trips that have to be taken. And as more and more people use home computer terminals, we will see a spreading out of the population. Of course, this won't happen overnight, but it is a long-term reality.

The computer is also being used for national planning: to set goals for the government just as private business does. An example is cash flow. Every business needs to know when its bills will come due, when payments are due, and when loans or other debts must be repaid. The computer can aid in the complex financial planning that must go into a business of any size. Proposed tax changes and other legislation can be tested on computer models of the entire nation with the result being, we hope, a more efficient and productive government.

Used correctly, the information on each and every one of us being stored in computer banks is of immense value. Used wrongly, however, it can lead to an invasion of privacy. The field of computer legislation and law is ripe for people willing and able to become involved in this area.

Whether we like it or not, societies have always had class divisions based on wealth, power, heredity, and other factors. Now a new class distinction will be added: those who have information and know how to use it, as opposed to those who don't. Power will be in the hands of the computer literate, those with credentials in computing.

Finally, worldwide communication and trade will be greatly improved with the use of computers. No longer will it take days to communicate properly with a business contact halfway around the world. Tedious, time-consuming paperwork will be reduced to minute-long transactions. International computing will be an increasingly important career area.

So the effects that the computer will have on society are molding the future right before our eyes. Where raw materials and financial capital were once strategic resources, knowledge will slowly take their place. Intellectual technology will replace machine technology in many areas. Our thinking will be directed toward information-based ideas rather than mechanical concepts. Future planning and productivity will require an ability to think into the future, as opposed to an orientation to what was in the past.

COMPUTERS AND BUSINESS

Not so long ago, we thought of computers, sheltered in climate-controlled rooms and staffed by "wizards," as the private domain of the largest corporations. This science-fiction image is now being completely replaced by science fact: computers are the domain of ordinary people, from one-person businesses to companies with hundreds or thousands of employees, each with his own computer terminal.

In fact, most experts predict that it will be next to impossible to stay in business in the next ten years without a computer. By 1990, a business without a computer will be as competitive as a business without a telephone is today. Even small "mom-and-pop" businesses! In all cases, computers will increase worker productivity (a serious problem in our country) by decreasing the time spent on routine tasks.

My situation is a case in point. I run a small one-man advertising agency. My personal computer takes care of billing, media insertion orders, receivables, payables, and more. This leaves me more time for what is the heart of my business and what I love to do most: designing ads.

No matter what the size of the company, the computer really can improve productivity. For instance, a business with only a few employees will utilize computers to manage finances, keep track of records and inventory, and prepare documents. Doctors, lawyers, accountants, and architects, as well as scientists and engineers, will use the computer to enhance their work and do away with routine, boring tasks.

The computer-connected systems of the future (the next few years!) will involve companies of all sizes connected by communications devices run by computers. In fact, some of these communications devices are in place now, including electronic mail. Sophisticated synthesized speech (words generated and actually spoken by the computer) is around the corner. The technology is available, ready to be implemented on a large scale.

On a larger scale, assembly lines will be moving toward even more automation, and employees will be retained for other, more interesting jobs. Animated films will be produced with the aid of computers, and the human voice will be used to enter data into computer systems.

In short, any organization involved in conducting business, whether for profit or not, will be revolutionized by the computer.

How will the computer be used? First, as a number processor, to continue to perform accurate and quick computations effortlessly. Second, as a data processor, to handle, process, and print huge quantities of data. Third, as an information analyzer, to aid and improve decision-making. And finally, as a knowledge processor, to make available to the public vast banks of information through electronic channels called networks.

Examples of these four major uses are: adding up the daily transactions at a bank (numbers processing); printing the charge account statements of a major department store (data processing); projecting sales for an industrial manufacturer (information analyzing); and planning a vacation schedule (knowledge processing).

COMPUTERS AND THE INDIVIDUAL

Most people are already deeply involved, either directly or indirectly, with computers. For instance, your name is on computer-generated mailing lists; your credit card purchases are processed by computers; and your airline and other transportation arrangements are made possible by computers. But what are some ways in which computers will be changing your life in the future?

First of all, computers will change the way people work. With home terminals becoming more and more popular, home work stations are foreseen for many employees, with the traditional five-day work week perhaps being split between home and office. With the popularity of these home work stations, the labor pool will be increased, allowing married women and men caring for small children to continue working. The 1980s will be the first decade when more people will work in offices managing information than in factories and other nonoffice work areas. The computer will help people continue to produce 600 million pages of computer printouts, 234 million photocopies, and 76 million letters *daily!*

In our homes, personal terminals will give people instant access to a wide range of information, including news, stock market reports, travel information, event schedules, and much more. Computers will also be used to balance checkbooks or prepare a household budget, as well as for hobbies, games, and entertainment.

People will be able to communicate with each other via computer and even send letters to friends. They will also be able to shop at home, receive tailor-made publications, and request information on almost any subject available.

Probably the biggest beneficiaries of computer technology will be children. They will be brought up in a computer atmosphere, and using computers will be second nature to them, just as watching TV is to most of us. Children already show an amazing tendency to become positively involved with computers, and whole new forms of learning will evolve as computers penetrate the classroom. Kids will spend more time programming their computers than watching TV—a delight to almost any parent!

That's only the beginning of a computer's use in the home. It will also be used for home controls: a computer will direct burglar alarm systems, stereo setups, and dishwashers and washing machines. And it will help the physically disabled, who now can feel a real part of society in computer careers. Not only will disabled persons be a part of the working mainstream, they will also benefit from the immense number of computer-oriented products that will help them communicate with other people more easily.

We can see how important computers will be in our lives. But the most important point is that computers will be everywhere. Computer careers will be available in every field, thus giving people the opportunity to follow natural interests under the umbrella of computing. For example, you might choose computers and hotels, computers and retailing, computers and finance, or computers and research. Wherever your interests lie, you will be able to prepare for and enjoy a career combining computing and your personal interests. No other field known to man can offer so much diversity.

What does the future hold for you? For those who are informed, employment opportunities will be fantastic. For those who are cyberphobic (fearful of computers) and who choose not to become educated or reeducated, our world will become an increasingly alien place to live. The point is clear: change with the times and you'll be in good shape. In fact, you may find that you become cyberphrenic—completely addicted to your computer terminal!

2. A BASIC PRIMER . . . NOTHING TECHNICAL

Now let's look at the computer itself: how it works, what makes up computer language, what the computer buzz words are, and how the computer is used in both routine and exotic ways. The background presented here is intended to give you a rudimentary understanding of how computers work. It is part of the total picture that is necessary for a smart decision involving your future.

With no further ado, here's a nontechnical look at how a computer works:

When you sit down at a computer, you type on a keyboard. The letters on this keyboard are usually identical to those on a typewriter, but there will be many additional keys with words like *return*, *reset*, and *ctrl* as well as some with special symbols. These keys are for specific functions, which you'll learn as you go.

The keyboard is your means of *input*, or getting information or *data* into the computer. Once the information is inside the computer, it is held in *memory* cells, waiting to be acted upon. A set of instructions or a *program* tells the computer how to *process* the information in its memory.

The results are then displayed on a television screen or printed on paper; this is the *output*. When you want to store programs or data, you do so on a *diskette*, a small flexible object similar to a 45-rpm record. When you need the programs or data stored on the disk, the computer calls that information from the disk back into its memory. The material is then ready for *processing*.

This is the general method a computer uses to process information. Let's look inside a computer to get a more concrete idea of the hows and whys.

When you type on the keyboard, each letter or number is converted into a series of 0's and 1's. This *binary* language is what the computer understands. The computer only knows 0's and 1's—nothing else—and because it is dealing with only two characters instead of dozens, speed and accuracy result.

After being converted into 0's and 1's, the data are then further changed into electrical impulses, which pass through integrated circuits and transistors, all on a silicon chip a quarter of an inch square. Each computer word, called a *byte*, is assigned a place in a memory cell to await processing.

The information, now in the memory cells, is acted upon and processed according to the program or instructions being used. The output, or final result, is then achieved and converted back into numbers and letters, which is displayed on the TV screen or printed on paper by a *printer*.

A computer's astonishing speed results from the quick movement of these electrical impulses in such a tiny space. Computer computations are in the millions-per-second range, and it's mainly because of the binary concept and the fact that the electrical impulses travel at nearly the speed of light.

A good programmer must be able to write proper instructions in the format that the computer can process. Programs, or the instructions for the computer, are developed as follows: First, the problem is analyzed, and a logical method to get from the start to the finish is thought out. It is then put on paper in the form of a *flowchart*, showing every possible alternative, i.e., if we come to point A and event 23 happens, then we go to solution C. (If you picture a branching tree you will have some sense of the flowchart.) There are literally thousands of possible routes through a program, which all depend on the information supplied and the choices available.

Finally, the programmer takes the flowchart and data and writes the line-by-line instructions so that the computer can process them. Here's a very brief example, a *statement* reading: 10 PRINT "my name is Irv." The elements of this statement include: the line number (10), an arbitrary number used to order statements; the command (PRINT), a word which instructs the computer to print (either on the TV screen or on paper) whatever follows; and quotation marks, which are one particular machine's way of identifying what you want printed, i.e., the words between the quotations.

Different computers support different *languages*, but the most popular language, one used in most personal computers is called BASIC. Many of the words in BASIC are in English, easily understandable even by us human beings!

There are many computer languages in use today. Each one was developed for a specific area. Languages like FORTRAN and ALGOL are used in science and engineering. COBOL is a business-oriented language and a language called LISP is used mainly in the field of artificial intelligence. Most of these languages go back to the mid-1950s or early 60s, and new languages will be developed in the future.

The difference between languages occurs in the way they are structured. Every character in a command (PRINT in the example above) takes up space, and hence time. Some languages that don't require easy-to-understand words might use a symbol Q1 for PRINT. This doesn't seem like much of a saving here, but is very useful when dealing with formulas and other special characteristics associated with that language.

A *Basic Primer . . . Nothing Technical* 13

   In preparing for a computer career, it is important to learn several languages, as each one can open up more doors for you. In the same fashion, it would be wise to get experience operating several varieties of computers put out by different manufacturers.

   Here are some other important computer terms; these are all you'll need to know to work your way through *Getting into Computers*.

ACCESS TIME: The time it takes for information to be retrieved from a memory cell.

ADDRESS: The actual location of a memory cell, which is used in the execution of a program. It also can identify the location of a storage cell.

ASCII CODE: The code for 128 upper- and lower-case letters, numerals, and special symbols, which are translated into 0's and 1's.

BIT: A "binary digit" (0 or 1), the smallest unit of data in a computer system. A BYTE is a set of bits, which forms a *computer word*.

BUG: An error in a program which has to be corrected for the program to work.

COMPILER: A technique or process that makes programs run faster.

DATA: Information that is fed into a computer for processing.

DATABASE: A collection of information arranged in a meaningful way.

DEBUGGING: The process of correcting errors.

DISK OR DISKETTE: The physical means of storing information and data. Disks are usually very hard and rigid while diskettes are flexible, commonly called *floppy diskettes*.

DISK DRIVE: A device that "reads" data stored on a diskette.

ENTRY: The beginning of a program or the point at which one enters data into the keyboard.

FLOWCHART: A graphic representation of the logical flow of events in a computer program.

HARDWARE: The physical components of the computer system—everything you see. (See SOFTWARE.)

INTERFACE: A device that connects and makes compatible two or more devices, such as a printer, typewriter, or telephone modem (hookup). (See PERIPHERAL.)

LANGUAGE: A system of representation and communication between the computer and people. Languages are available on all levels for specific purposes.

LOOP: A series of instructions that requests the computer to perform whatever instructions are inside the loop for as many repetitions as is desired.

MEMORY: The part of a computer that holds data and instructions, usually for a short period of time. Permanent memory is "written" onto disks or diskettes.

MICROPROCESSOR: The actual "brains" of the computer, which takes data from memory, instructions from the program, and processes the two and prints a result.

OPERATING SYSTEM: Instructions by which a computer functions.

OUTPUT: The result of processing, which is displayed on the TV screen or printed on paper.

PERIPHERAL: Any device that is interfaced to a computer is a peripheral. Examples include the television monitor screen, a telephone modem (hookup), a clock, or a voice box.

PRINTER: A device for printing the output from a computer onto paper.

RUN: The computer command that sets a program in motion.

SCANNER: A device that scans or transmits the contents of a piece of paper into a computer for storage.

SOFTWARE: The actual set of instructions or a program that tells the computer what to do. (See HARDWARE.)

SYSTEM: The broad term for an overall method of achieving a goal, which combines various hardware and software elements.

WORD: A group of usually 2, 4, 6, or 8 bytes.

8 Bits to a Byte

A word about computer words: You may have overheard these words used in conversation, especially by teenagers who are computer aficionados. The remarkable thing about words in BASIC is that they really are easy to understand. One need not be afraid of them, or, for that matter, of any part of the computer.

Take, for example, a word like *peripheral*. You probably have heard this word used before, and knew it meant "near to or around a central object." It's easy to see why the word was chosen to describe accessories that work outside of the computer. With most of these words, you don't have to look for hidden meanings to understand what they mean.

After you use the words for a week or two, they'll become second nature, and you'll find yourself explaining them to people who are now in the position you used to be in!

There are other computer words that are even more graphic or exotic in nature but are based on reality. These include:

CRASH: When a computer breaks down (not often) it is said to "crash." The trick is how fast it can be made to work again. Many times the problem can be solved over the phone with today's personal computers.

DAISYWHEEL: This is a modern-day improvement in high-speed typewriters, named after the flower because of its design. Instead of keys, a round plastic or metal disk, imprinted with letters and numbers, spins around to the desired spot. When it stops, a hammer presses the sliver

A Basic Primer . . . Nothing Technical

of the daisywheel onto the paper. It is then released, spins to the next character, and is hammered again.

DOWNTIME: Sounds like a new rhythm, but it's not. It refers to the amount of time a computer is "down" or not in operation due to a crash.

JOYSTICK: Here's a naughty-sounding word to describe a device necessary to most games. It is a little stick which a game player moves around to make the shape(s) on the screen move. It's a source of "joy" to people who use it. Hence, joystick!

MOTHERBOARD: No, it isn't what you're thinking. It's a type of circuit board, into which many different boards or interface cards can be plugged.

There are many fun words in computing; these are just a few. You'll discover a whole bunch of them as you get started.

3. LOOKING AHEAD: COMPUTER APPLICATIONS TODAY... AND IN THE FUTURE

We've previously seen how computers will affect society as a whole and you individually, but now let's get specific. We'll now look at actual applications, a popular computer word used to define what a computer can do in any given setting.

The marriageability of computers to every field will account for the tremendous career opportunities for you. You'll have your choice of computing and medicine, computing and journalism, etc. So it is important to know about the wide variety of opportunities and applications—from the routine to the exotic. This knowledge will give you more information to help you better analyze your future in computing.

I will cover applications by areas—computers in science, education, communications, etc.—with each area containing many uses for the computer. Read through them all—not just in an area you might currently be interested in. But remember, this is just a sampling and by no means a complete list.

COMPUTERS IN COMMUNICATIONS

Quite possibly the largest area of computer involvement is communications. Communications refers to the electronic transmission of information—whether by television, satellite, cable, or by a telephone linked to a computer. The applications here are endless, with new developments appearing daily.

We all will eventually communicate with others by computer. We will send communications and other documents by computerized "electronic mail" over thousands of miles in seconds. Businesses already are heavily into transmission of documents, plans, reports, and other printed matter over the telephone lines.

The television set is one device that has saturated the American public's homes, and it will be a major channel in the future for computer-driven systems. You will be able to electronically scan the morning newspaper and select articles and ads you wish printed out on paper. You will be able to view and buy products using your home computer terminal and TV, and you will also have access to many forms of information on a wide range of subjects.

In fact, the whole country will be interconnected with networks of data and information. (Many of these "nets" are already operative.) Information will be available instantly, at almost any time of the day, and without time-consuming reference.

Computers will continue to change the face of publishing. Many major newspapers now have their entire editorial staffs writing into computer terminals, editing their articles right on the screen and "sending" the articles over to the editors' computer terminals. Correspondents all over the world can file stories at any time for editing back home. Only when the article is written, edited, and approved is it ready for typesetting, which, of course, is done electronically through a compatible computer hookup.

Magazines will also face many changes, one of them truly fascinating. You'll someday be able to receive a magazine tailor-made to your tastes and preferences. If you like horseback riding, stamp collecting, gourmet cooking, and jogging but dislike smoking, movies, and rock 'n' roll music, your editions of *You* magazine would contain articles and ads about what you like, and spare you articles and ads for what you don't like. You wouldn't be bothered by ads for cigarettes, movies, and rock concerts, since the marketers of these products aren't interested in reaching people who don't want to smoke or dislike movies anyway!

Advertising will also change. With more information available on people's likes and dislikes, advertising can be better targeted to people likely to buy the product. Advertising and marketing will therefore become more efficient and less wasteful.

Professional writers, both free lance and those employed by publications, will use word-processing equipment to speed up and enhance their writing. In fact, this entire book was written on an Apple II computer with word-processing peripherals (remember that word!). The day will come when a writer will go to his publisher and hand his editor a floppy disk and say, "Here's my manuscript!" There are even software programs out now that go through an entire book or article and correct any spelling errors, all while you're having a cup of coffee.

The yellow pages of your local phone book will take a different shape. You'll be able to access listings right from your home computer terminal, thus effecting an enormous savings in directory assistance personnel. Already computers "talk" with voice messages such as telephone-programmed responses. An alternative to directory assistance will be having your directory inquiry handled by computer, with an artificial voice giving you the number you need.

Computer owners now have the ability to communicate with one another by simply dialing a "bulletin board." Available on a wide range of topics, from astronomy to comedy, these bulletin boards have posted messages, which you can simply enjoy or add to. Passwords are used, and you can have a great deal of fun in addition to making "computer friends" that you never actually speak with.

The first generation (the initial production) of portable computers is already available. You can pack these machines up and take them with you, even on overseas business trips.

Entering information by speaking to the computer is already technically feasible. In addition to entering data on a keyboard, you can talk into a microphone connected to the computer, which now recognizes a limited vocabulary; someday it will understand an infinite number of words.

Other forms of communications and presentations will use the computer and television to negate the distance between people and to make communications more advanced than they are today. One example is teleconferencing. The meeting of a board of directors can now take place even if every director is in a different state! Photos are compiled on a giant screen so everyone can see each other. Voice lines are connected, and computers at each location can print out paper copies of necessary documents.

Some new condominiums have personal computers as a standard feature in every unit, hooked up to an information-retrieval network. Now that's progress!

COMPUTERS AND SCIENCE

Computers will continue to aid scientists in every area. Computers got their beginnings in science and continue to be at the heart of scientific research and production, whether it's research on the composition of Mars or the development of technology for a new machine or automobile.

Computer chips are starting to appear in cars to control brakes, doors, and speed; display information on gas mileage and arrival times; and even to provide personal reminders and messages. All forms of transportation now use computers; the automatic pilot is one good example that has been around a long time. Ships' radar and navigational information are computer assisted, and the new high-speed railroads have their routes mapped and monitored by computers.

Engineers are using the computer for dozens of projects. Electrical engineers use it for analysis of complex problems. In concert with scientists in other disciplines, engineers are studying the way man thinks and how our brain controls emotion, memory, muscles, and imagination. Civil engineers use computers to map out homesites to retain the land's natural contours and vegetation while making the best use of the space available.

Cameras now have computer chips to control the electric eye and shutter, in order to get even better quality. Film processing is computerized, which results in a more consistent developing of your vacation photographs.

Medicine is another area where computers have made and will continue to make major breakthroughs. Huge data banks on every illness known to man are now available, making analysis and treatment much easier. Doctors can consult thousands of case histories in minutes, giving the patient the benefit of many years of combined experiences and treatments. Potential adverse reactions to drugs can be flagged by the computer, which can have the patient's allergic reactions and other characteristics on file. Before seeing the doctor, patients can give their medical histories to a computer as well. These computer interviews are done in English, French, and Spanish, with an instant translation available for the doctor. This computing technology is currently in use in over forty-five hospitals and medical and nursing schools in the country, with many more planning to follow suit.

Psychological therapy and the treatment of mental illnesses will be aided by the computer, something no one ever dreamed of before. Many patients already feel more comfortable about answering questions coming from a computer than from a person. For some reason, they open up more because they feel the computer won't judge them. Computers can even form a tentative initial diagnosis. When this diagnosis is combined with the doctor's or social worker's assessment, a more efficient and perhaps better treatment program can be implemented.

Scientists have developed a computer chip which can help women identify their infertile periods. The chip measures variations from normal temperatures and transmits this information to a visible digital display. Eventually computerized devices will even be able to be implanted inside our bodies to monitor and react to heart stress and other problems.

COMPUTERS AND BUSINESS

We're all familiar with computerized credit-card bills, airline tickets, mortgage and bank statements. We've seen for years how businesses use computers for financial transactions, mailing lists, and keeping records.

Now, new methods and devices are enabling businesses to become even more efficient and better organized. Computers can assist firms in long- and short-range planning, examining everything from capital requirements to personnel needs.

For instance, employee performance on the job can be monitored to increase productivity and pinpoint problem areas. This is done by analyzing thousands of work hours, noting the slowdown periods and places where they occur. Productivity is a major problem in this country, and computers can help identify the problems and suggest solutions to the productivity dilemma.

Aside from "number crunching," computers will also help business analysis through the use of graphics, charts, and tables, visible on a TV screen in a multitude of colors. Complex companies with many subsidiaries will be better able to visualize profit centers and loss areas with computer graphics capabilities.

Electronic banking has the potential to cut down on the immense flood of paper in this country. Billions of checks could eventually be replaced by electronic transactions, thus eliminating problems of bounced checks for insufficient funds. For instance, if you went to a store to purchase groceries, your account would be punched in, and the amount of the order electronically deducted from your account and added to the store's. If you did not have enough money in the account, it would be up to the store to cancel your order.

Stock-market transactions are, of course, already computerized, but now the individual investor can reap the benefits of computer technology. You can gain access to major financial reporting services to get instant stock quotes on your home computer. You can even have your portfolio of securities updated on a daily basis.

Computers will change smaller businesses, too. At your corner drugstore, for instance, your prescriptions along with other relevant information, such as your allergies, will be stored on a computer. Bulky files will be eliminated; updated information will be available in an instant.

Businesses and organizations use computers regularly and in greater numbers than most segments of the population as a group. This imbalance will slowly even out as the general public gets into the act, but businesses will continue to need qualified personnel to keep computers humming.

COMPUTERS AND EDUCATION

Computers will revolutionize the educational process, beginning at the elementary-school level. The young people of today are already being brought up in a computer-literate world and use computers as

Looking Ahead: Computer Applications Today

easily as a recent generation used pocket calculators and typewriters. Learning with the help of computers is becoming second nature to them.

The whole process of learning is being reevaluated in light of the computer's awesome power. Different modes of learning are being developed, with the result that teachers who are computer literate are needed desperately.

Learning in the classroom using the computer involves a high level of instant feedback and positive strokes for correct answers, and gentle corrective words and repetition for incorrect answers. The student moves at his own speed, punching in answers and getting rewarded as fast as he wishes.

Computers stimulate thought and keep students' attention because they help make their textbooks come alive. For example, students from many schools around a state can participate in a mock election. Assuming the schools can communicate with one another via a computer linkup (which is currently feasible in many schools around the country), they can then simulate an election. They'll set up "local" political headquarters, tabulate votes by using census information and even conduct polls of fellow students. The result of this gives all the students who participate a very realistic look at how elections work, one which is made possible through participation rather than by memorizing the information.

Experts predict that because young people adapt so well to computers, a serious national division could result: eventually, our country may be run by the computer literate, with people who have resisted involvement with computers almost helpless to participate successfully. It is important that people of all ages become involved with computers in order to prevent this situation.

Libraries are currently being interconnected by computer channels, making their resources available to people all over each state and even throughout the country. Published resources can be located instantly with a computer terminal. A list of these resources can then be transmitted from one location to another and even printed on paper—all while you wait! Books can be catalogued on computer index files. Because the amount of printed information continues to multiply at a pace that threatens storage space, it is possible that in the future publications will be stored completely inside computers.

A $50 million network of computers already unites nineteen colleges in California, leading to more course offerings and sharing of resources.

As the world moves toward computer literacy, computer education becomes more and more important. Computer courses are now becoming mandatory in high schools and colleges. The state of Minnesota is way ahead of the rest of the nation: 97 percent of its high school graduates have had some exposure to personal computers.

The only way to survive in the computer age is to educate our young from the beginning. The field of education will require people to develop educational programs and hardware, teachers on all levels to implement them, and, perhaps most important of all, parents to provide encouragement.

COMPUTERS AND SERVICES

In addition to rapidly becoming an information society, we are also becoming a service-oriented society. The number of people employed in all kinds of services is increasing dramatically compared to the number involved in production of tangible products. People in the service category include lawyers, doctors, architects, plumbers, hair stylists, package-delivery services, repair people, advertising and promotion agencies, mailing-list houses, and many more. People involved in these diverse occupations all have one thing in common: they provide time, labor, and knowledge for their remuneration instead of a product you can see and hold.

The computer has made great strides in assisting service-oriented businesses. In service businesses time is most important, and the computer has freed valuable time for the more important aspects of the business. Every hour an accountant or stock broker spends doing routine and nonproductive paperwork (which can be handled by a computer) is an hour lost. This time would be better spent in soliciting new business or in developing existing accounts. My advertising business is all service, and the computer has given me more time. The same is true for almost everyone in any service occupation.

Lawyers have had a tremendous boost from the computer with the development of programs that store and catalogue information on precedent-setting cases. Lawyers can now punch in some simple codes to obtain relevant information on a specific case in order to help them better pursue the case at hand.

For instance, say a lawyer's client wants to sue a car dealer in another state who he claims sold him a defective automobile. To obtain precedents and related information on what is now an interstate matter, the lawyer can enter keywords such as "automobile," "car dealer," "interstate," and the names of the states involved. The computer will search all the cases, attempting to find instances in which two or more of these words appear in the same case transcript. The case name, file number, and date then appear for further referencing, as well as the entire text if requested. This replaces hours upon hours of painstaking work by law clerks, and increases the likelihood of finding appropriate cases by a substantial margin.

Government is basically made up of many agencies providing many services. Without computers, there would be no government in this day and age. It's true that fifty years ago there were no computers capable of today's immense performance, but there were many fewer people, agencies, and numbers to keep track of. Without computers, the work force of the government would probably have to triple—if not become even larger!

To keep track of and administer programs such as social security and welfare, the government has more computers and computer employees than any other single entity. As long as there is a government, there will be a continued demand for computer people at all levels of government service.

Individual politicians also use computers, to keep track of their constituents and what they've said or written on specific issues. Political fund raising is a massive mail-order business, impossible without computers.

Truckers and all kinds of shippers are currently connected by computer to improve efficiency. A trucker with an empty rig can instantly find a broker who needs a load shipped to the trucker's destination. The result is fewer empty trucks and improved service.

The retail store is being quickly updated by sophisticated computers. With every purchase, a retailer, large or small, can keep track of inventory and profits. He can tell at a glance which items are moving, which are sold out and need reordering, and what his sales/profit/expense picture is at any moment in time. Exciting careers will be forged in this area as people start to shop by home computer and video.

Many of the skilled trades are being computerized. Printers, for example, use computer typesetting equipment that cuts time and cost by an amazing factor. The ever-changing cost of paper and printing labor can be programmed to make it easy for printers to give price quotes. In the same fashion, electricians, plumbers, and builders can keep track of major jobs, inventories, and expenses. Once again, the computer frees time for the more important aspects of service businesses.

COMPUTERS AND ENTERTAINMENT

Probably one of the most well known areas of computer involvement is entertainment. There will be many new and exciting applications in the years to come.

We're all familiar with computerized games, toys, and puzzles, whether the hand-held variety or the larger arcade machines, or even the ones that hook up to your TV. The computer chip is inside the spelling games that you can hold, the adventure game that has lights, action, and sound as well as any game that produces digital readouts or other exciting graphics.

Computer technology is responsible for the cheapness of these games and their instant popularity. More and more complexity is being built into them, with musical sounds, flashing lights, and even talking becoming standard fare. The development, marketing, and retailing of these games is now a gigantic industry, one sure to continue to grow.

There are other areas of entertainment where the computer has made its mark, notably in what many would call the "fine arts." Musicians now use computers not only to compose, but to create and shape sounds, many of which have never been heard before. One of the unusual sounds, for example, is like a gong shrinking in size during the duration of a musical note. The computer's versatility enables the exact repetition of a musical piece, precise down to the last note, as well as putting a whole musical composition into orchestration in the confines of your home!

Artists too have been getting into the act. Computer graphics is a rapidly growing field, and a gallery specializing in computer graphic arts has opened in New York. Artists can "call up" shapes (such as a tree viewed from the inside out) and then program the images to move, rotate, change hue and color intensity. Animation, once a laborious job of hundreds of individual scenes, now uses a computer to fill in the frames and create continuous action.

In tournaments involving the thought games—bridge, chess, and backgammon, to name a few—computer entrants are doing very well. Computers on the grand master's level can take a few days to analyze each of millions of combinations possible before a move is made. You can play these games with a computer by yourself, with a partner or a trio.

For years Hollywood's special effects, most notably in the science fiction movies, have counted on the computer to create effects which are literally out of this world. One example is the black hole, an effect that is hard enough to imagine let alone to create. Another is the computer-generated graphics, characters, and movements found in many of the science fiction movies. Computer graphics in movies enable the producer to create illusions and scenes otherwise impossible, such as a nuclear explosion seen from the inside of the fireball.

Even love is not left alone by the computer. A California minister created a computer program to perform a wedding ceremony, where "I do" meant pushing the "y" for yes button. He even had an answer should someone press "n."

With all the applications being developed at a dizzying pace, the point is very simple: it's now possible to combine a career in computing with the love of your life, no matter what it is.

Since computers are found in almost every field, from art to steel production, the choices are as varied as your imagination. And since most experts predict the overwhelming presence of computer technology in this country, it almost becomes impossible *not* to be involved with them.

The term or label for this is, of course, computer literacy. It would have seemed absurd, even two years ago, to say that artists and musicians should be computer literate. But they should be, as should retailers, accountants, and every other career-oriented person. Now let's take a look at the organization of the computer industry.

4. THE EMPLOYMENT SCENE

The following headline from a general daily newspaper aptly summarizes the current computer employment situation: "The Computer Industry is Hungry for Skilled Workers." To put it plainly and simply, computer companies are crying out for qualified individuals in order to make a $60 billion industry into a $600 billion one. The shortage has lead to severe cases of competitive headhunting among companies, as well as to extravagant bonuses and perks for new employees. In fact, you could even call new recruits who are on the ball "bonus babies."

Computer companies are spending a lot of money on employment firms and newspaper advertising because they must get highly skilled workers who want to grow along with the company. But they will turn down people who think they can slide in on a wave of employment fever without adequate preparation and training.

The computer industry may be short of personnel now, but as people recognize this, the number of new graduates will increase, and there will be periods of time when entry-level jobs may actually be hard to find. This is true in any industry experiencing rapid growth as many people try to get on the bandwagon.

There are two schools of thought on the employment situation in the computer field. One holds that the field is already experiencing some overcrowding. But the other school of thought, the one I believe in, says that the computer industry is still tiny, with room for immense growth, and hence more jobs. And of course more and more companies are entering the field as more areas open up.

Companies are starting to "grow their own" computer personnel by training secretaries and clerks who know the firm and have already developed a sense of loyalty to it to be programmers and analysts. These firms take successful employees seriously.

The picture is quite rosy for those interested in computing as a career. And the need is not just for technical people, but for personnel across the board. Computer firms need a full complement of people in management, advertising, marketing, production, shipping, accounting, personnel, data processing, and so on.

The list of employees needed by these firms is too long to include fully here, but I will summarize the most important and commonplace categories in the job descriptions section. In addition to the employment opportunities in computer companies, there are many openings in companies that use computers, called end-users. Since almost every company that's not a computer company is an end-user, common sense tells you that there's a huge number of them.

The servicing of computers will be an important career area. Since businesses come to depend heavily on the computer for their daily transactions, whenever the computer "goes down," everything stops. And well-trained people to provide trouble-shooting service are needed critically. Computer companies without the ability to solve problems quickly will be way behind their counterparts who keep "down-time" to a minimum.

Another great need will be for people to teach computing on all levels. We will need men and women who can teach computing at the elementary, high school, and college levels. And since most computer manufacturers and software houses run seminars, classes, and tutorials on using their equipment and products, teachers will be needed in industry, too.

The number of publishing ventures sprouting up to support the computer industry is already becoming impressively large. There are now over 130 publications, many glossy 500-page booklike magazines, with more introduced every week. Because there are so many facets of the computer industry and computers to cover, there will be more new publications, too. Obviously, good writers, artists, production people, advertising people, and the rest of the usual publication personnel will be needed to produce these periodicals.

So when you imagine the computer companies themselves, the end-users, and all the support firms, you can see that there are an enormous number of possibilities, with an even larger number of openings. Getting a job, if you're qualified, shouldn't be a problem; making an intelligent, meaningful choice is your task.

Take the most commonly known job in computing: the programmer. By 1990 the demand for programmers will double, creating about 250,000 new positions. Entry-level programmers with four years of college in computer science or related fields generally start at about $20,000! On-the-job training is intense, and a company must invest an average of fourteen months to train each employee. With these costs in mind, computer firms aren't hiring just anybody off the street. They want only good, qualified people, and will pay for them.

An offshoot of the traditional programming sector of computing is contract programming, where programmers work free lance for a fixed rate. San Francisco, along with other growing metropolitan areas, is a hotbed for this type of activity.

Unfortunately for computer firms (but probably fortunately for those programmers who can make it as contract programmers), the rate of pay is much higher for contract people. This prompts company programmers to leave firms and set up businesses of their own. This is an unhealthy situation, as it serves to drive costs up, and I hope that with more and more programmers graduating, this disparity will fade. However, you should be aware of this possibility in your future.

A contract programmer usually runs his own business, which doesn't initially have the benefits, such as group insurance and profit sharing, found in most larger firms. Furthermore, the contract programmer must provide his own public relations and advertising. To feel secure in your own business, you must be a special type of person. For a programmer who is essentially shy or introverted, contract programming is probably a poor choice.

As with all career opportunities presented in this book, I urge you to look at the total picture, and not jump at large potential income while ignoring other, perhaps more subtle, benefits or drawbacks.

For instance, one subtle drawback in many computer jobs is less social interaction. In the past, in order to complete a transaction, one might have had to call several people, meet with others, and contact one or more departments. But the computer takes away much of this face-to-face transacting and telephone calling. Since more information is available at the touch of a button, people talk to each other less on the job. This can cause stress, which must be dealt with. (It might be a good idea to bring this topic up in an appropriate class, and maybe even do a project on it, such as a term paper. It's an area not mentioned often, but one of increasing importance.)

Another rapidly growing computer sector is the so-called programming cottage industry, with technical specialists developing software at home! Entrepreneurial consultants, free lancers, and small firms are taking advantage of this mode of working. Yet another distinct possibility in your future.

One of the most fascinating and rapidly growing areas which deserves a separate mention is CAD/CAM, or Computer-Aided Design/Computer-Aided Manufacturing. The computer is used to form a valuable link between the electronic brain and the mechanical hand. Simulations and models can be used to visualize almost any three-dimensional product, from a bearing assembly to a complete truck or tractor. People in this young sector of the computing industry are being overwhelmed with all this new technology, and understanding it and communicating it to today's workers is a challenge.

There are enormous profits for companies involved in CAD/CAM, and exciting career opportunities. CAD/CAM is excellent for someone mechanically inclined who may want to investigate working with computers in manufacturing.

Everything is not all peaches and cream in the world of computers, and whenever there is dissatisfaction in any field, lawyers and lawsuits are not far behind. In fact, litigation involving computer companies is one of the fastest-growing concerns of both the legal and computing fields. A legal career involving computers may be just right for you.

In any industry there will be misrepresentations, faulty equipment, or problems that the vendor doesn't correct. One would hope that these problems are no more prevalent in the computing industry than they are in any other industry. However, when there is a problem with a computer the consequences can be serious and far-reaching. A business that keeps its entire records on computer is faced with calamity should the computer break down, malfunction, or lose some of the data or information. A firm that buys a $20,000 system only to find it will take two years to properly program it won't be enthusiastic about computers after having to wait so long.

Because computers are proliferating so fast, the field of legal computing is evolving very quickly. Lawyers are developing specialties such as software piracy and equipment performance expectations.

One of the most heartwarming benefits of computers is what they make possible for physically disabled people. Both in education (discussed in a later chapter) and the career workplace, disabled people are finding jobs in computer programming and related jobs. To be a successful programmer, you need a sound, logical mind and persistence; people with physical problems are by no means restricted in their computing abilities. In fact, in a recent study, it was shown that the physically disabled did as well as or better than their healthy counterparts in work productivity.

By now you must be wondering: "But where do I start? With all the options available, how do I make sense of it all?"

Since logic is one of the chief characteristics of computer people, we'll answer this question logically in the next chapter, by looking at the basic career sectors in the computer industry.

But before we examine each of these career areas more closely, let's take a look at salaries, increases, geographical factors, and employment trends for the industry as a whole.

EMPLOYMENT TRENDS FOR THE 80'S IN THE COMPUTER INDUSTRY

50 percent. 40 percent. 77 percent. 75 percent. 18,659 percent. 80 percent. 90 percent.

In case you haven't guessed, these figures refer to growth in various sectors of the computer industry. Growth and employment have been healthy, and a look at the statistics might give you a clearer picture of the potential for the industry as a whole.

The employment of computer workers as a group increased by 50 percent during the 1970s, to over 1.2 million workers. This rate was 2.5 times the rate of growth for most other occupations analyzed for government reports.

A combination of technological advances and changes in the methods of operation have resulted in different rates of growth within the computer industry. Programmer employment grew at 40 percent, more slowly than the 77 percent growth of systems analysts, the people who do the logical thought behind computer systems. The rate of growth for service technicians was 75 percent, but the largest increase, at over 100 percent, was for computer and peripheral equipment operators, the people who run the machines. This was due to the sheer number of new installations.

One company's growth pattern illustrates a curve that is perhaps typical—and certainly something to envy. Tandem Corporation, a computer manufacturer, grew 18,659 percent in four years. Sales jumped from $581,000 to $108,989,000. But the big story for future computer workers was the rise in employees at Tandem. In 1976 Tandem employed 71 workers; in 1978, 446, a sixfold increase; and just two years later, 1,387 employees. As companies continue to expand at phenomenal rates, computer workers will be in more and more demand.

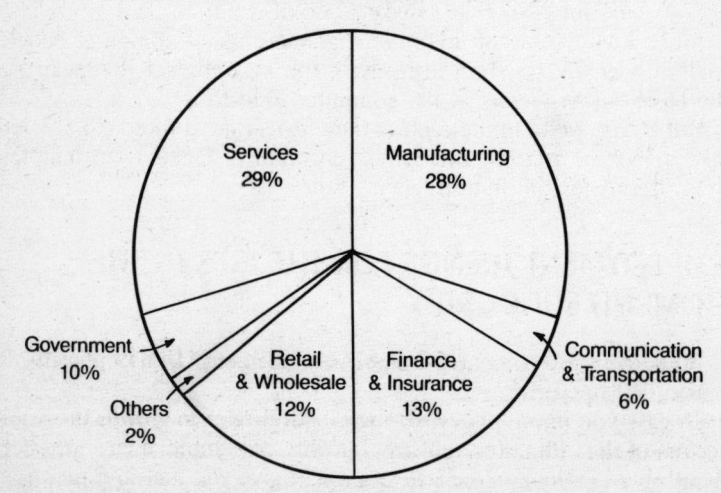

Where computer people are found, by fields

- Services 29%
- Manufacturing 28%
- Government 10%
- Retail & Wholesale 12%
- Finance & Insurance 13%
- Communication & Transportation 6%
- Others 2%

Overall projections for now through the end of the eighties are for 80 percent growth for the field, or almost four times the rate for all other occupations. Employee availability is not keeping pace with expansion; hence the current demand for new, qualified people. Service technicians are pegged at 150 percent growth; systems analysts at 120 percent; and programmers at 100 percent. Keypunch-operator growth is declining, because of the ease of data entry on television screen monitors as opposed to the now old-fashioned computer cards.

In terms of actual numbers of people, a rise to 2,140,000 computer workers is predicted by 1990. Systems analysts are expected to hit 400,000; programmers, 500,000; computer and peripheral equipment operators, 850,000; service technicians, 160,000. As mentioned before, the number of keypunch operators will decrease from 273,000 to about 230,000.

In a more general sense, the total information sector will grow to over 44 million people, or about 47 percent of the work force. Agriculture and industry are both declining to a combined 25 percent share, with services accounting for the remainder.

SALARIES

Entry-level computer science graduates can expect to earn about $20,000 or better to start. Salaries rise quickly with experience and are also influenced by the size of the company and the geographical location.

Oftentimes the total remuneration package is more important than the amount on the weekly paycheck. Stock options and profit-sharing arrangements may prove to be very valuable, since many of these companies experience rapid growth. Other hidden financial benefits, such as expense accounts and the use of company cars, can account for substantial dollars that are not taxable. You should shoot for the best financial package, which may not necessarily have the highest salary.

WHERE THE JOBS ARE

It is easy to tell you the areas where computer jobs are found today, but don't let that mislead you. Not only is the industry changing fast, which means expansion and movement into other geographical areas, but the nature of the computer itself will account for a further spreading out of employment opportunities. Since one computer can instantly communicate with other computers, companies can now afford to locate satellite offices and plants in areas where taxes are low, i.e., away from big cities and expensive suburbs. So any attempt to predict the future areas of concentrated employment would be foolish. Instead, I think it's safe to assume geography will not be a major factor in your career search.

However, you should know what some of the hottest locations are right now. A cluster of towns in California with very pleasant-sounding names—Sunnyvale, Cupertino, Redwood City, Palo Alto, Santa Clara, Mountain View—has become a focus for the computer industry. Dozens of firms manufacturing computer hardware, especially tiny circuits, have located here, accounting for the area's nickname, "Silicon Valley." Outside this obviously rich computer area, the growth nationwide is occurring both in the big cities (end-user sites) and in suburban areas (computer manufacturers, plants, and support services).

New York State, with a decided emphasis on New York City, leads the nation both in demand and in salaries, while Connecticut, California, and Nevada are 5 percent above the national average. These are current trends, but as companies grow and need more space, they tend to look into cheaper land and tax bases, which means away from metropolitan areas.

In other states (Florida, Maine, North Carolina, and New Mexico) computer industry growth is currently lower than the national average. They have their own peculiarities, such as older populations or sparser numbers, which influence companies investigating settling there.

The top eight states by number of estimated computer installations (end-user sites) are California, Illinois, New York, Pennsylvania, Texas, Massachusetts, Michigan, and Ohio, according to 1981 information.

Other hot areas will be Alaska and Hawaii, because of their remoteness. People will be paid a premium to move to these out-of-the-way places.

That, basically, is a very rough picture of the computer industry with regard to employment increases, salaries, and projections. The individual sectors and job titles will carry their own salary information.

PART II
CAREERS WITHIN THE COMPUTER INDUSTRY: JOB DESCRIPTIONS

5. THE FOUR CAREER AREAS

Careers in computing exist in two distinct areas: within the computing industry as designers, developers, manufacturers, and packagers of computer products and services; and outside the computer industry as end-users.

Part III of this book will focus on computer careers outside the computer community, while this section will look at careers within the industry. Since complete descriptions and salary ranges will be presented here, they will be omitted in Part III. This is because the jobs analyzed in careers outside the computer industry, or end-users, are the same as or similar to the careers presented in this section.

There are four major areas that make up the computer industry; companies involved in one area may also be involved in others.

The beauty of the industry is its lateral flexibility. As a programmer, for instance, you're not locked into the same type of company forever. Because programmers are needed in a variety of companies, you can probably work either inside the industry or for an end-user. And you can usually switch from one to the other.

Additionally, you can move among the four areas described below should there be a demand for your type of talents. And you can take additional credits to learn about other areas that involve more responsibility or demand different job requirements.

DESIGN AND MANUFACTURING

People employed in this area are concerned with designing, developing, and producing computer hardware (the actual physical components) and software (the instructions or programs to run the hardware). This section is by far the largest of the four, encompassing every type of company, from the one-person garage operation to the major corporate entities such as IBM, Digital, and others.

These companies design and build computers, printing devices, accessories, and electrical components to further enhance the original machines. They create and write the software and instruction manuals and provide training seminars and tutorials for their products.

As a group, the design and manufacturing segment represents at least half the total number of jobs in the industry.

SERVICE, MAINTENANCE, AND INSTALLATION

While design and manufacturing presently have the most employees, I believe this group will be the fastest growing in the years to come. As the number of computers installed increases dramatically every year, more and more people will be needed to service the machines in the event of breakdowns.

Routine maintenance and service is sometimes provided by the manufacturers themselves, as well as by independent companies. Independents can sometimes have the advantage of providing a faster service, which is critical when all of a firm's records are on the computer.

The other area examined here is composed of the people who install computers, who can either be employed by independent companies or sent directly by the manufacturers. People employed in this area of the computer industry have the responsibility of making sure all the hardware performs the way it should, taking into account factors like climate, electrical wiring, and so forth.

WORD AND DATA PROCESSING

This segment of the computer industry offers a service: the processing of words or numbers for businesses of all kinds. Your corner drugstore, whose statements come to you via a data-processing house, is one example of a firm utilizing this service. A firm using word-processing services is another.

In general, word and data processing firms offer the benefits of a computer's power and speed to companies who can't afford their own or don't want one, for any number of reasons.

The jobs found here are those associated most with processing data—keyboard entry, operators, and the like. People in this area take in raw information, process it, and deliver meaningful documents to their clients.

SALES, MARKETING, AND RETAILING

This final area is concerned with the selling of computers and the marketing of computer products and services. It encompasses the following: publications that serve the industry, retail stores that sell computers, representatives of companies that manufacture computers, independent sales and marketing consultants and firms, mail order houses, direct marketing organizations, and so forth.

People who work in this area become expert at marketing computers, whether the personal microcomputers or the giant mainframes.

Each class of computer requires a totally different marketing strategy, and people develop expertise in the various markets and distribution outlets that have become available.

AN IMPORTANT NOTE ABOUT JOB TITLES, DESCRIPTIONS, AND SALARIES

If you talk to five different people in the computer field who do essentially the same job, you'll probably get five different job titles and salaries. Computer personnel sometimes have similar titles but do different work and make different salaries.

In order to make some sense of this conglomeration, I've averaged out information to create these job titles, descriptions, and salary ranges. It is doubtful that you'll find any one job title that exactly fits the description found. If that were the case, this book might be thousands of pages thick.

Therefore, the job titles are generic and can't be construed to mean that the title at hand is the only title for that description. Other titles are usually given within the text.

Job descriptions are generic, too, since each company will add or subtract duties and responsibilities from those I have presented here. In terms of salaries, the range presented should cover most instances, but again you can expect some variation from company to company, or in different geographical areas.

6. DESIGN AND MANUFACTURING

As mentioned earlier, this area is the heart of the computer industry, from which come computer hardware, software, accessories, and electrical components. This area is diverse, covering every type of position from designing the circuits of a computer's memory board to writing the code for a business software program; from assembling a keyboard to developing a computer that can talk.

Within the design and manufacturing segment of the computer industry there are two major divisions: hardware and software. The hardware part of the industry is concerned with producing the physical components of computer systems. Some examples of the elements produced in the hardware sector are: computer chips, which are circuits of electrical components designed to manipulate impulses at high speeds; circuit boards, which connect and combine chips, electrical components, and other devices to achieve specified purposes; disk drives, which "read" the information stored on diskettes in the same way a tape recorder plays back a tape; monitors, which are TV-like screens that display the information the operator is working with; and a voice synthesis mechanism, which allows you to talk into a microphone and have your words translated into computer-understandable language for inclusion into a computer program.

The key factor in the hardware sector is that you can hold or see the final product. It is either a personal computer, a chip, a giant mainframe, or one of hundreds of other designs. But it is a tangible product made up of components combined to achieve a certain goal.

On the other hand, software is more intangible: often you can't see it. It is lines of code on tape or diskettes, which are meaningless to most people. You know that a software program will accomplish certain goals via the instructions written in code on the diskette or tapes, but you can't look at it or hold it, as you would a bar of soap or bottle of soda. You don't get your pound's worth with software, although you do get user manuals (instruction books), which are, usually, quite hefty. What you are paying for, instead, are the "brains" to make the hardware run effectively and accomplish the highly specific tasks required.

People who work in this area are charged with first producing a flowchart of the program by analyzing the company's needs and showing a logical means to achieve goals presented. Then the program has to be written in code, in one of many computer languages, so that the computer will understand the instructions and carry them out. Software people must also produce user manuals which instruct the end-users in the operation of the program and explain the various options open to them.

Though hardware and software people have very different jobs in terms of what they produce and how they go about it, they are linked to each other in a marriage that will never dissolve. One can't work without the other. All the hardware in the world couldn't work without the software to run it. And the finest software programs, taking years to develop, aren't worth a dime unless they have the proper hardware to run on.

This marriage of hardware and software accounts for the fact that many jobs in the two sectors overlap; obviously there have to be excellent communications between the two to assure compatibility in hardware and software.

The career summaries that follow have been organized primarily by hardware and software. Those careers that can be found in both areas are indicated as such. When you read about these careers, it is important to think about them in the total context of the hardware/software arena, with the purpose of combining your ideas and goals with the way this segment of the industry is structured.

I'd also like to point out that in hardware companies you'll find both sales and marketing jobs, as well as service, maintenance, and installation careers. These careers will be discussed in Chapter 7.

Additionally, of course, you will find careers in hardware firms that are not computer related: accounting, secretarial, shipping, etc. These careers, since they are not truly computer careers, have not been treated here; you might consult *The Career Finder*, another title published by Ballantine Books.

HARDWARE CAREER SUMMARIES

As previously mentioned, the hardware sector of the computing industry is concerned with creating and making the computer systems and accessories. In addition to production operations requiring assembly lines and raw materials, there is much design work involved in getting the system to function properly. To this end, the hardware sector is organized into four distinct sections.

RESEARCH AND DEVELOPMENT

Engineers and designers experiment with new logic design, circuit construction, and component development to create new products making use of advanced technology.

ENGINEERING

The people working in this department, which is sometimes part of the R & D group, take the plans developed by research and investigate the raw materials that will make the hardware function best. They have to analyze everything, from silicon chips made by different manufacturers in the U.S. and abroad to the plastic casing, power supply, and other components of the total system. They also must purchase limited quantities of these components to create a prototype. Finally, they must make sure that the materials they choose will be usable in a mass-production line.

PRODUCTION

The people here are concerned with setting up and operating a plant with assembly lines to mass-produce a hardware product. They take the prototype developed earlier, analyze all the components, and set up the procedures to mass-produce it at the most efficient cost and best possible quality.

Since computers are so costly and perform vital work, there is no room for errors or poor products. Production people specializing in testing/quality control develop test procedures, specifications, and standards to make sure mass-produced hardware will function properly.

A separate group of specialists writes the necessary instructions, or "operating systems," which the various pieces of hardware require in order to run. Operating systems are internal machine-oriented instructions that users of computers are rarely concerned with. This differs from software, which are instructions or programs designed to accomplish a particular task.

TRAINING/ADMINISTRATION

People in this area oversee the education and training of a company's employees and conduct classes for end-users of the firm's products.

RESEARCH AND DEVELOPMENT POSITIONS

DESIGNER

A designer is concerned with the research and development of new hardware products. Logical thought, combined with intensive researching culminates in the preparation of a prototype—a working model—for further analysis and testing. This phase of a designer's work takes about 80 percent of the time, while documenting the de-

Design and Manufacturing

sign in writing and providing detailed specifications take up the remainder.

RELATED TITLES: Senior or junior designer.

ADVANCEMENT: The designer is the first rung on the research-and-development ladder, to be followed by engineer, project manager, and R & D manager. One can become a consultant in this area further down the line.

EDUCATION: A minimum of a bachelor's degree in computer science or engineering is necessary; a master's in engineering is desired.

EXPERIENCE: Two or more years as a technician or draftsman (see The Production Area, p. 44) is also helpful.

PERSONALITY: A thorough person who doesn't mind working alone and can handle mental pressures associated with concentrated technical work would be well suited for this position.

ENVIRONMENT: Most of the work is in an office setting, usually in a larger size firm; opportunities for advancement without additional training are limited, but there is a lot of personal satisfaction to be gained. Supervision is minimal.

TRAVEL: Minimal.

SALARY: The range is $15,000 to $25,000, which varies with the designer's experience and the size and location of the institution.

INSIDE INFORMATION: You can often work after hours or on your own time as a designer; the pace is steady and the competition isn't intense. This job is a real challenge for the creative thinker and technically oriented person.

ENGINEER

The engineer works with the designer in developing a new hardware product. The actual development work (the physical creation of the hardware) uses up about four-fifths of the engineer's time, with the remainder split between writing specifications and supervising other engineers and draftsmen. The job can also involve investigating, specifying, and purchasing parts, components, subassemblies (circuit boards, keyboards), and production equipment. Time is split between working with other people and working alone, and there is usually off hours work because much thought and creative problem solving are required.

RELATED TITLES: Senior, junior, associate, or assistant engineer.

ADVANCEMENT: The engineer is second on the career path after designer, and before project manager and R & D manager. Consulting is also a future possibility.

EDUCATION: A bachelor's degree in computer science or engineering with appropriate computer credits in hardware and logic is necessary.

EXPERIENCE: The entry-level position is as an assistant. Full engineer status requires two plus years as an assistant or designer.

PERSONALITY: A thorough, logical individual is desired.
ENVIRONMENT: The office is the central work area.
TRAVEL: About 20 percent of the time is spent traveling, in order to find and analyze new components, attend seminars, and represent the company.
SALARY: The range is $18,000 to $35,000, and can be increased by having an MBA, which would give the worker additional management skills. The salary will vary according to the size and location of the company and the experience of the engineer.
INSIDE INFORMATION: The pressures on this job are strictly mental ones due to the technical nature of the job. This is another challenging position, perfect for an intelligent person who likes a steady pace and can work well without supervision. There are many job opportunities here, plus the choice of working in large or small firms.

PROJECT MANAGER

A project manager coordinates all the aspects of a particular assignment. The management and supervision of engineers, designers, and technical people accounts for 70 percent of this job. Keeping up with the technical end, to be better able to make an overall decision, accounts for the remainder of work time. The project manager is usually responsible for the development of a complete product line (many related items) or one specific piece of hardware.

There is a considerable amount of overtime and at-home work in this position, along with day-to-day deadline pressures. There is plenty of contact with fellow workers, and this position has high visibility, can provide much personal satisfaction, and offers solid financial rewards.

RELATED TITLE: None.
ADVANCEMENT: The project manager follows designer and engineer on the corporate ladder, with further management positions next in line.
EDUCATION: A bachelor's degree in computer science is necessary, and an MBA most helpful.
EXPERIENCE: Two or more years as a designer and/or engineer is acceptable, and production experience is quite useful.
PERSONALITY: A well-poised, well-groomed person who is a good leader and manager of people is necessary.
ENVIRONMENT: There is much interaction with subordinates in the office setting, and the project manager occasionally rolls up his sleeves to work alongside his fellow workers.
TRAVEL: About 10 percent of the time for meetings and seminars.
SALARY: Between $20,000 and $40,000, depending on the location, size, and experience.
INSIDE INFORMATION: Politics and power enter into the picture here;

this is much more than a technical management position as the pace is fast and constantly changing, with other people always angling for the manager's spot. This spot requires a hard-working person with a thick skin.

MANAGER—R & D

The research and development manager oversees the entire R & D operation, usually coordinating the development of all new hardware product lines for a company. The management end of his job takes up about 80 percent of his time; the balance is spent in keeping up with technical changes.

This is a plum position, offering challenging work, much personal satisfaction, and financial reward. For these reasons, it is competitive, and the right person spends much time at home keeping up with the latest technological advances.

ADVANCEMENT: The position of R & D manager represents the culmination of many years in the research and development area. It has high corporate visibility, and other management positions are accessible from this spot.

EDUCATION: A bachelor's degree in computer science or a related engineering field is necessary; an MBA is desired.

EXPERIENCE: One would need two plus years as a designer and engineer and several years in production as well.

PERSONALITY: Good leadership qualities are necessary.

ENVIRONMENT: There is much interaction through meetings and conversations in the office setting.

TRAVEL: About one-fifth of the time is spent away from the office in attending seminars to keep abreast of new developments.

SALARY: From $30,000 to $50,000. Company size, location, and the manager's credentials affect these figures.

INSIDE INFORMATION: The ideal R & D manager works as well alone as with people and writes and expresses himself well, especially to management who are not as technically oriented as he. Given the nature of the computer business today, there is pressure upon the R & D department as a whole to come up with newer and better products, which inevitably become the manager's responsibility.

CONSULTANT

A consultant can work for one or more firms and is called in for a specific assignment which can be short or long in duration. If he works with several different customers at the same time, he hops from client to client, working on different projects.

He may work with designers at one company, advising them of new

or different ways to create desired hardware; with engineers to perfect a prototype; or he may assist writers in developing the final documentation or working manuals. Eighty percent of his job is technically oriented, with the remainder spent in preparing documentation. Some supervision of other consultants in a large company may be called for.
RELATED TITLE: None.
ADVANCEMENT: A consultant is an above average person who either strikes out on his own (running his own business on a contract basis with firms requiring his services) or joins a consulting firm which will market his services.
EDUCATION: A bachelor's degree in computer science or engineering with appropriate credits in hardware and logic design is needed.
EXPERIENCE: Over six years experience in product design, engineering, and testing is needed in order to be able to advise a firm.
PERSONALITY: He should be outgoing, thorough, and logical. He must also be able to keep one step ahead of most other people to be in continual demand as a consultant.
ENVIRONMENT: A consultant usually has temporary office accommodations at one or more of his clients.
TRAVEL: Depending on the length of the assignments, travel may occupy from half to three-fourths of the time.
SALARY: Between $25,000 and $50,000, with higher earnings possible for really good people. A consultant "gets around" and sometimes can later join a company at a good salary because of his experience there through consulting work.
INSIDE INFORMATION: Due to the fact that some consultants own their businesses, the amount of time spent with them increases. In addition to their consulting work, they must take care of taxes, bookkeeping, billing, and advertising and promotion. The good consultant must be able to get along with all types of people without flaunting his intellectual advantages. The consulting arena is as competitive as it is fast-paced, with independence, financial reward, and being your own boss desirable premiums.

THE PRODUCTION AREA

Up to this point, the jobs covered have been exclusively hardware oriented. Since hardware and software are so intertwined, many of the careers in the balance of these chapters can be found in both hardware companies and software firms.

TECHNICIAN

The technician has to understand the logic of circuits (combinations of electrical parts and wires) as it applies to specific equipment being developed by his employer's company. Half his time is spent in that endeavor, and the other half is spent in wiring, testing, troubleshooting, and repairing equipment or products.

In this position a person spends a lot of time working alone and in many cases puts in considerable paid overtime. Not only are there deadline pressures in this job, but there is also physical pressure due to the smallness and closeness of the work.

RELATED TITLE: Senior or junior technician.
ADVANCEMENT: This is a limited position and a basic entry-level job. With additional training, however, there is more possibility for advancement.
EDUCATION: A high school diploma with an associate degree in a particular technical area is necessary.
EXPERIENCE: None required.
PERSONALITY: An alert person with good finger dexterity is ideal for this position.
ENVIRONMENT: The work of a technician is performed either in a plant or machine-type shop, usually in a large firm.
TRAVEL: None.
SALARY: The range is $10,000 to $20,000, depending on responsibilities, experience, and location and size of firm.
INSIDE INFORMATION: The pace here is steady, and the work that has to be done is usually well defined and structured, good for someone who needs direction. Personal satisfaction can be gained from seeing a complex electrical mechanism perform millions of computations per second. The financial reward here is not astounding—hence the opportunities are pretty wide open.

FABRICATOR

The fabricator is involved in the actual nuts-and-bolts assembly of hardware products. This nine-to-five position includes securing components onto a circuit board, wiring, testing, and repair. All work time is spent with these duties, with no technical or written tasks required; while there are other people on the assembly line, you essentially work alone. As in most assembly-line jobs, major tensions stem from the day-to-day deadlines of meeting quotas. The pace is steady, and you won't find much competition for these positions, which are almost exclusively found in large firms.

RELATED TITLES: Machinist, tool maker, core assembler, board wirer.
ADVANCEMENT: Advancement is limited to the next title, line supervisor. College credits could help one advance beyond that point.
EDUCATION: A high school diploma with the necessary trade school credits or an associate degree is required.

EXPERIENCE: None. This is an entry-level position.
PERSONALITY: Good finger dexterity is required, with patience for repetitive tasks helpful.
ENVIRONMENT: The work is performed in a plant, on an assembly line, or in a shop.
TRAVEL: None required.
SALARY: The range is $10,000 to $20,000. This figure varies with location, size of firm, and experience.
INSIDE INFORMATION: Fabricators can get a lot of personal satisfaction from knowing they contributed to one of the most complex and effective tools ever developed by mankind. The salary may not be exceedingly high, but this job will appeal to someone who enjoys the security of a steady job that will be around for years to come.

LINE SUPERVISOR

The line supervisor's prime responsibility is just what the title implies: to supervise the assembly line, making sure that there are no production snags. There is also a fair amount of hands-on assembly work where required, some need to keep up with the latest equipment and procedures, and a high degree of interaction with workers on the line doing varied jobs. A line supervisor must be sharp, know every procedure inside out, and be able to handle day-to-day deadline pressures.
RELATED TITLE: Supervisor.
ADVANCEMENT: This position is the first step on the management ladder, with advancement possible (with additional experience and education) to engineer, project manager, or even manager of production.
EDUCATION: A high school diploma is required.
EXPERIENCE: Two years or more as a fabricator or similar position is needed.
PERSONALITY: This person must have leadership abilities in order to relate with coworkers.
ENVIRONMENT: Most of the work takes place in the plant or on the assembly line. A supervisor usually has an office.
TRAVEL: None required.
SALARY: The range is $15,000 to $25,000, dependent on size of company, experience, work record, and location.
INSIDE INFORMATION: There is a degree of power and political influence in this position, plus the personal satisfaction that can be gained from managing people and machines. The opportunities are limited as this is a supervisory job, and as a result competitive. While the pay isn't overwhelming, this can be a springboard to better engineering and management positions.

Design and Manufacturing

ENGINEER

The engineer in the production department spends about 70 percent of his time developing new techniques for production and acquiring new equipment, materials, and parts. The rest of his time is spent in overseeing other engineers, technicians, or fabricators, and with manual work involving special tooling and sophisticated equipment.

This is one position that is found in both the hardware area and the software sector, but varies with the type of products being produced. It also involves both working alone and with other people.

RELATED TITLE: Senior, assistant, associate, principal or test engineer.

ADVANCEMENT: This position, the second on the production ladder, can lead to management positions—project manager or manager of production—with additional credits or experience.

EDUCATION: A bachelor's degree in mechanical/electrical engineering with credits in computer science is desirable.

EXPERIENCE: Two or more years as a technician. This can be an entry-level position (as an assistant engineer).

PERSONALITY: A thorough, logical person will do well in this spot.

ENVIRONMENT: The work is split between the plant and office.

TRAVEL: About one-tenth of the time is spent traveling.

SALARY: From $15,000 to $25,000, depending upon experience, educational credits, location, and size of firm.

INSIDE INFORMATION: An engineer must be able to absorb day-to-day pressures, which often necessitate bringing work home. This can all be worthwhile, as the position has intellectual status in the computing community. The demand for engineers is high, making competition less of a factor than in other positions and giving the candidate many different opportunities. Much personal satisfaction can be gained from this challenging position.

PROJECT MANAGER

The project manager is responsible for the production of a specific hardware (or software, as this is a position found in both areas) product or line, from tooling to fabrication to assembly and testing. For 60 percent of the time, he oversees the production or project team. He splits the rest of the time between hands-on troubleshooting and keeping up with technical changes and new equipment.

This career requires working closely with people in many different areas and on many levels, from technicians and fabricators to management. As a result, the project manager must have the ability to communicate on these many different levels.

RELATED TITLE: Product manager.

ADVANCEMENT: This position follows line supervisor and engineer, and is the step before manager of the production department.
EDUCATION: A bachelor's degree in computer science along with an MBA is preferable.
EXPERIENCE: Two or more years in engineering and design is desirable.
PERSONALITY: The project manager should be outgoing, able to lead and coordinate, and capable of working well with other people.
ENVIRONMENT: Time is split between office and plant.
TRAVEL: About 10 percent of the time, to keep abreast of changes.
SALARY: $18,000 to $35,000, depending on experience, size of company, and location.
INSIDE INFORMATION: There is some power attached to this job, as well as enjoyable travel and pay benefits. Because it's a good position, offering high corporate visibility which can lead to even better positions, it is highly competitive. A position to strive for.

MANAGER OF PRODUCTION

This is the top spot on the ladder in the production department. The manager oversees the work force, usually with the assistance of certain key personnel or supervisors. This overseeing accounts for most of the manager's time, but there is some shirt-sleeves work and time spent on updating his technical knowledge.

This is the position that represents the culmination of years in the production area, offering a good salary, bonuses, and high corporate visibility among upper management. Because of these benefits, the position requires long and sometimes uncompensated hours, as well as additional pressure due to increased responsibility.
RELATED TITLE: None.
ADVANCEMENT: This position has high corporate visibility, and can lead to other management positions within the corporation. It's also vulnerable—one bad mistake can cause termination from this spot.
EDUCATION: The minimum requirement is a bachelor's degree in computer science or engineering; an MBA is highly desirable.
EXPERIENCE: Four plus years in engineering, project management, and design are usually necessary.
PERSONALITY: A well-poised, even-tempered person who gets along well with people.
ENVIRONMENT: The time is split between the office and plant.
TRAVEL: There is minimal travel, perhaps between plants or to seminars.
SALARY: Between $20,000 and $40,000, depending on the size of the company, its location, and the diversity of the production department.

INSIDE INFORMATION: The pace here is steady in terms of day-to-day activities but involves considerable 'keeping on top of things' in order to retain the position. This position is found mainly in larger hardware firms.

THE TRAINING/ADMINISTRATIVE AREA

TECHNICAL WRITER

The technical writer spends his time in writing, editing, and proofreading the various materials that accompany the hardware and software products his company produces, from user manuals (how to use a specific software program) to the installation instructions of a complete system. He must be technically competent and able to write clearly. At this level, there are no management or supervisory responsibilities. The work is steady-paced.

This position involves a high degree of communications ability; since the technical writer has to communicate highly technical material in an easy-to-understand manner. As a result the job provides a certain degree of intellectual satisfaction.

RELATED TITLE: None.
ADVANCEMENT: This is a first step toward the eventual goal of education and training administrator, which will follow course instructor.
EDUCATION: A bachelor's degree in computer science with credits in journalism and English is needed.
EXPERIENCE: Several years as a programmer is desirable.
PERSONALITY: One must be organized for this position.
ENVIRONMENT: Usually an office setting.
TRAVEL: Minimal.
SALARY: The range is $15,000 to $25,000, varying with company size, location, and experience.
INSIDE INFORMATION: The technical writer essentially works alone. The pressures of this position are strictly mental, involving a lot of searching for the exact words to describe a process or procedure. Since good technical writers are scarce, opportunities for finding work are abundant. Personal satisfaction is a major benefit of this job.

COURSE INSTRUCTOR

The course instructor spends most of his time conducting and teaching classes for company employees and end-users of the firm's products. These educational seminars cover many aspects of the products and are viewed as highly important by the company.

Course instructors are found both in the hardware and software areas, and are a vital link between departments in terms of communicating the abilities and limitations of a product.

RELATED TITLE: None.

ADVANCEMENT: This position is one notch above that of technical writer and, with proper training and experience, can lead to other management positions. There is good corporate visibility here.

EDUCATION: A bachelor's degree in computer science with advanced credits in teaching is good preparation. A master's in teaching is even better.

EXPERIENCE: Several years in systems analysis, programming, and technical writing is appropriate.

PERSONALITY: One must have good oral-presentation skills, be able to handle large groups, and be well poised.

ENVIRONMENT: The time is spent in the office and classroom; there is much after-hours preparatory work involved.

TRAVEL: Depending upon where the company has its offices located and how many course instructors it employs, travel can be minimal or substantial.

SALARY: $20,000 to $35,000, depending on location, size of firm, and number of classes taught.

INSIDE INFORMATION: The long hours required for course preparation are compensated for both financially and by a sense of intellectual satisfaction and status. Because there isn't much competition for this position (the abilities needed here are not common), there are many opportunities with a wide array of companies and products.

EDUCATION AND TRAINING ADMINISTRATOR

This person oversees the education and training of a company's employees. Heavy emphasis is placed on molding an employee into the firm's unique way of conducting business, and to that end, much time (up to two years in some cases) and money are invested in employee training.

Most of the time in this position is spent in making assignments, developing schedules, solving problems, and administering new courses.

Found in both hardware and software firms, this job offers high corporate visibility and personal satisfaction, as the position (similar to that of a course instructor) is vital to a large number of employees.

RELATED TITLES: None.

ADVANCEMENT: This position is the top rung in the education and training area. It can lead to other management positions, as well as to positions in other divisions of the firm.

Design and Manufacturing

EDUCATION: The minimum required is a bachelor's degree in computer science or related field, with credits in business courses. An MBA would be quite helpful.

EXPERIENCE: Having had experience in programming, technical writing, and other areas, the E & T administrator should possess an overall knowledge of the entire process, not just expertise in one area.

PERSONALITY: This person must be organized, thorough, and able to delegate work effectively.

ENVIRONMENT: Most of the time is spent in the office, with many meetings and phone conversations.

TRAVEL: Limited, depending on company locations.

SALARY: From $20,000 to $35,000, depending on location, size of firm, and experience.

INSIDE INFORMATION: The E & T administrator enjoys some political power, but has to work to keep it. Day-to-day deadline pressures and relationships with many people throughout the firm must be juggled effectively. Creative approaches are needed in order to put together effective training programs and develop new teaching methods. This position is found mainly in large firms. Few job opportunities exist, as you don't find many E & T administrators in any one company.

SOFTWARE CAREER SUMMARIES

The software industry is the counterpart of the hardware sector. People involved here write the programs and instructions for the computer to execute. While in hardware the emphasis is on producing a tangible product, here it is on creating instructions to achieve a certain goal.

The software industry produces a wide range of programs, from programs for games that may involve graphics and other creative formulations to complex scientific and business applications. The end package is usually composed of one or more diskettes or tapes with the program(s) on it, a detailed user manual, and other special instructions.

The process of initially taking a problem, defining a goal, and working through to the end result, a workable program, involves three general steps: planning, system designing, and programming. Planning involves the establishment of general specifications for new software programs. System design involves taking general specifications and producing a detailed system design including flowcharts and documentation. Programming translates the previous work into the actual code (program instructions or statements) needed to run the new application.

People producing software can sometimes be found in hardware firms or in retail stores. The career summaries presented here, however, are those of predominantly software-oriented companies. Other careers involving software will be covered in later chapters.

There are basically five divisions within a software firm, which correspond to the available work areas:

RESEARCH AND PLANNING

People here define the needs or requirements of a new system, work up a general design, perform an analysis of the end-user's requirements, and review methods of achieving the stated goals.

DEVELOPMENT

Here the actual system is designed. This includes the creation, writing, and testing of the programs, installing the new system, training personnel, and writing instructions. This area has the most job titles.

MAINTENANCE

Generally, software needs to be continually updated, so this department reviews proposed application changes, design modifications, or rewrites, tests the new versions, modifies the instructions, and trains or retrains personnel if required.

PRODUCTION/OPERATION

The people here run the programs on the equipment for which it is intended as well as prepare input—keypunching or data entry—for the program.

TRAINING

People in this area research education needs, develop courses for data-processing personnel, conduct classes, and prepare text material. Continuing education and seminars for end-users are very important areas for software companies. Because the field is dynamic and constantly changing, the need to "be on top" of new developments almost always affects the firm's sales.

RESEARCH AND PLANNING POSITIONS

SOFTWARE DESIGNER

A software designer creates operating systems (methods by which the computer can function), compilers (technical programs that aid the efficiency of the system), and utilities (special features), duties that occupy about 80 percent of his time. The other time is spent in document writing, drawing charts, and supervising small groups of programmers or analysts.

This is an intellectually challenging position, requiring much steady-paced work alone on complex programs involving many different branches and pathways. The need to get software finished as soon as possible to beat out competition can create deadline pressures.

RELATED TITLES: Software engineer.

ADVANCEMENT: This position is first in this area, and without more education is limited. With additional training, one can advance into management positions such as project manager or manager of planning.

EDUCATION: A bachelor's degree with heavy computer credits is required; an MS in computer science is desirable.

EXPERIENCE: Several years in application (business or scientific) programming is desirable; systems design experience would be helpful.

PERSONALITY: A stable, organized, and methodical person with an even temperament is perfect for this position. Management qualities are not necessary.

ENVIRONMENT: A professional office atmosphere is the usual setting.

TRAVEL: Minimal.

SALARY: The range is $15,000 to $25,000, depending on experience, responsibility, and company location.

INSIDE INFORMATION: Personal satisfaction in this job can be high, since the designer is given freedom to define work areas and approaches.

SYSTEMS ANALYST

A systems analyst is responsible for designing new systems and applications based on a given need in a business area. (For example, a firm might require a program to keep track of service and repairs on its fleet of cars.) The technical aspect of his job (60 percent of his time) is combined with management and supervision responsibilities (30 percent), since he is responsible for coordinating small groups of analysts or programmers working on a project. The remaining 10 percent of his time is spent on written material, including charts and manuals needed as part of the overall system design.

While a software designer creates specific programs and routines (parts of a program), an analyst looks at the whole picture. For this reason, he needs to work closely with many people on different levels as well as to put in time working at home.

RELATED TITLE: Planning analyst.

ADVANCEMENT: The systems analyst (responsible for the overall *approach* to a problem) is second on the path after software designer (responsible for the actual programs needed for the analyst's approach method), and following this title are senior and chief analysts and management positions.

EDUCATION: A bachelor's degree with computer credits is required.

EXPERIENCE: Several years in programming (good college experience can be acceptable) using high-level languages like COBOL, FORTRAN, and BASIC.

PERSONALITY: A poised person who functions well under pressure is desirable. Other important traits include good oral and written communicating ability, leadership qualities, and being a good listener.

ENVIRONMENT: A professional office is the setting.

TRAVEL: About 10 percent of the time is spent traveling for committees, trade shows, and contact with vendors.

SALARY: The range is $20,000 to $35,000 per year, which varies with duties, size of firm, location, and experience.

INSIDE INFORMATION: This job provides intellectual gratification, whether the job is found in a small or large firm. While this is not a big moneymaking position, it is an important stepping stone and many opportunities exist for advancement, especially for an analyst who is versatile.

PROJECT MANAGER

The project manager, found in both software and hardware firms, is responsible for groups of professionals up to about thirty people in size. His major goal is to coordinate all the tasks involved in producing a specific software applications system or hardware product. Additionally, he must be technically competent and up to date. Therefore, about a third of his time is spent keeping abreast of the state of the art.

Here is a position with high corporate visibility and a commensurate salary.

RELATED TITLES: Project leader, project director.

ADVANCEMENT: This position is a managerial one, and it can lead to that of manager of planning or other positions in corporate management.

EDUCATION: The minimum required is a bachelor's degree in computer science or a related field; desired is an MBA. or equivalent experience.

EXPERIENCE: Several years in systems analysis and programming with high-level languages (COBOL, FORTRAN, BASIC).

PERSONALITY: Management traits are needed for this position—good poise, communication skills, leadership ability, and self-control. The project manager should be dynamic and fairly aggressive.

ENVIRONMENT: There is considerable interaction in meetings, presen-

tations, and phone conversations to complement a professional office setting.
TRAVEL: About 20 percent of the time, for committee work and vendor contact.
SALARY: From $25,000 to $40,000, depending on company and department size, as well as location.
INSIDE INFORMATION: There is take-home work in this position, as the pace is fast and there are constant changes in business philosophies, corporate policies, and technical developments to be kept up with. Since this job offers both good pay and the possibility of advancement, the competition is keen, requiring long hours which may not be directly compensated. A good project manager can exert some power.

MANAGER OF PLANNING

This is the top spot in the research and planning department of the company, whether it's software- or hardware-oriented.

The manager has responsibility for his department, both for the many people in it and the many applications in process. This dual responsibility accounts for most of his time. He also needs to have some involvement in a technical area in order to be able to make better decisions.

Since he has political power and is highly visible to upper management, the manager of planning is a person who must perform on a daily basis. From this stem daily mental pressures and the need to do plenty of at-home work.
RELATED TITLE: Director of planning (and research).
ADVANCEMENT: This position has high corporate visibility and can lead to other management positions in different departments.
EDUCATION: The minimum requirement is a bachelor's degree in computer science or a related field; most desirable is an MBA with computer credits.
EXPERIENCE: Several years in system and/or programming areas is necessary, with two years as a project manager.
PERSONALITY: This person must have good poise even under pressure. Oral and written communication skills, the ability to deal effectively with people either in large groups or one-on-one, and leadership qualities are desirable.
ENVIRONMENT: A professional office setting.
TRAVEL: About one-fifth of the time, for research, committee work, and vendor contact.
SALARY: From $30,000 to $50,000, depending on the size of the firm and the planning department.
INSIDE INFORMATION: This, as with most management spots, is a

highly competitive position, with few job opportunities in large firms and fewer still in smaller companies. Though the pace is steady, the responsibilities are substantial. The project manager interacts with many different people and on many different levels. The job is taken home and lived with constantly.

CONSULTANT

Consultant is not a typical position in a corporation, but is definitely a job possibility for a sharp person. He usually works under the customer's direction or under that of a technical manager, spending most of his time in designing system requirements, analyzing customer needs, and documentation and technical writing.

Whether he works in the software area or on hardware projects, he has considerable paid overtime opportunities and enjoys intellectual status, travel, and financial reward.

RELATED TITLE: None.

ADVANCEMENT: This position is limited in terms of advancement, but if one is a successful consultant, he is not really interested in working for someone else.

EDUCATION: A bachelor's degree in computer science or related field is a basic requirement; an MBA is desirable.

EXPERIENCE: To be a consultant, you need over five years in data processing (systems analysis and design) and two to three years in programming.

PERSONALITY: Frequent job hopping necessitates the ability to work well with different kinds of people in many different settings.

ENVIRONMENT: A consultant works at a client's facility, usually in an office, which sometimes may be makeshift and not entirely comfortable.

TRAVEL: Most of the time a consultant travels between clients, and frequent relocation is one of the aspects of a career in this area.

SALARY: The range is $30,000 to $40,000 or higher depending on the consultant's experience and reputation. There are also good benefits plus the bonus of owning one's business.

INSIDE INFORMATION: Both mental and physical pressure are constants in this position. A consultant is required to be creative, and to define his own work areas and approaches to problems. Since much time is spent in travel, there is limited growth potential due to the lack of time available for consulting. He may even have to live in a city for weeks or months away from home in order to complete a job. Finally, the consultant has to cope with the special pressure involved in running one's own business. This position requires a very special individual who can adapt well to different people and circumstances.

Design and Manufacturing

DEVELOPMENT POSITIONS

CODER

This title is practically extinct as programmers in many companies now do their own coding.

The coder spends most of his time coding programs—converting specifications to a code that the computer can understand—by following precise guidelines provided by the programmers. He may also do some program design.

This position is found both in software companies and hardware firms, mainly in large ones that can afford coders in addition to programmers. It's a nine-to-five job with little take-home work, and requires a person who likes working alone most of the time.
RELATED TITLES: None.
ADVANCEMENT: Progression into programming is dependent on one's ability and desire to get ahead.
EDUCATION: Required is a high school diploma with a minimum of an associate degree or other technical programming training.
EXPERIENCE: This is an entry-level position.
PERSONALITY: A coder must be detail-oriented and orderly.
ENVIRONMENT: The work takes place in the office, with terminal equipment for encoding.
TRAVEL: None.
SALARY: Between $10,000 and $18,000.
INSIDE INFORMATION: The job is steady, routine, and very structured, not allowing for creative approaches. One can gain personal satisfaction from translating requirements received in English into complex codes a computer will be able to understand. But examine a coder's job before you take it to see if it can lead anywhere else in the firm. Because of the trend away from using coders, you don't want to be caught in a dead end.

DOCUMENTATION LIBRARIAN

This person organizes, files, and keeps track of system documentation, instruction manuals, and other written materials pertaining to systems developed by the various computer departments.

In both large software and hardware firms, this individual enjoys being able to place his finger on any materials desired by people within the company. This is an eight-hour-a-day job, with no at-home work to speak of, and little if any pressure.
RELATED TITLES: Senior, chief, or assistant documentation librarian.
ADVANCEMENT: Progression is limited to library work, but with additional courses, one can progress into programming.

EDUCATION: A high school diploma is required; some computer courses, either in college or trade school, are welcomed.
EXPERIENCE: This is an entry-level position, but any data-processing experience is helpful.
PERSONALITY: This individual must be organized and methodical, as well as being capable of manual labor (filing, etc.).
ENVIRONMENT: The work is performed in the computer operations library.
SALARY: A documentation librarian earns from $10,000 to $20,000, depending mainly on the size of the library and workload.
INSIDE INFORMATION: Since this is a very calm and steady job, the right person here should be more concerned with security than financial reward. This isn't a highly competitive job, and a number of job opportunities exist.

TECHNICAL WRITER

This position involves the actual writing of instruction manuals, documents, operating procedures, and specifications for the end-user. There might be some involvement in the design and implementation of a system.

The ideal person in this position, whether he is writing for software or hardware, should work well in a structured environment within a large firm. There isn't much take-home work, and much of his time is spent working alone.

RELATED TITLES: None.
ADVANCEMENT: This position is limited, because the writing field does not provide much growth potential unless combined with other assignments in business or management areas.
EDUCATION: A bachelor's degree in computer science is necessary; advanced degree credits in writing, teaching or other related areas are helpful.
EXPERIENCE: Two years in programming would be most helpful, but not necessary.
PERSONALITY: A good command of the language coupled with fine-tuned communication skills is needed.
ENVIRONMENT: The work is done primarily in the office.
TRAVEL: Minimal.
SALARY: Technical Writers earn from $12,000 to $25,000, depending on workload and quality of work, location, and company size.
INSIDE INFORMATION: While there are some deadline pressures, usually the pace is steady, without the peaks and valleys of other positions. There is a degree of intellectual satisfaction to be gained here, as writers are the communicators, the explanatory link between hardware or software and the end-user.

PROGRAMMER (BUSINESS)

A business programmer spends most of his time in program development, writing, and design for business applications such as accounting, financial forecasting, data-base management, etc. This person should be well versed in COBOL and BASIC, the high-level languages used primarily in business. Additional time is spent on program coding and documenting.

The business programmer can gain much intellectual satisfaction from developing heavy-duty programs which hundreds or even thousands of businesses will use. He works alone much of the time, but finds it a real challenge.

RELATED TITLES: Senior, junior or lead programmer; analyst/programmer, assistant programmer.
ADVANCEMENT: This position is a normal first step in the progression through the programming ranks, leading to systems analysis jobs and eventually project management.
EDUCATION: Required is a high school diploma plus a minimum of an associate degree in computer programming; desired is a bachelor's degree in computer science or related field.
EXPERIENCE: This is an entry-level position for a junior or assistant programmer. Two to four years is required to reach senior programmer.
PERSONALITY: One should be organized, logical, methodical, patient, and even-tempered.
ENVIRONMENT: A programmer uses computer terminals to work in an office setting.
TRAVEL: Occasionally for seminars, schooling, and trade shows.
SALARY: $12,000 to $25,000, depending on firm's need for quality programmers, location, and experience.
INSIDE INFORMATION: There are mental pressures here due to the technical nature of the work, as well as deadlines which may require take-home work or late hours. This position is a stepping stone for future good positions, whether in a small or large firm. Many job opportunities exist, though career growth potential as a business programmer only is limited.

PROGRAMMER (SCIENTIFIC)

Like the business programmer, the scientific programmer spends most of his time in program design, development, and writing. However, this position requires knowledge of the FORTRAN, BASIC, and/or ALGOL high-level languages, since the applications here involve scientific principles, formulations, and theories. Twenty percent of the time is spent on coding and documenting.
RELATED TITLES: Senior, junior, lead, or assistant programmer.

ADVANCEMENT: This position is limited to advancement into systems analysis, with additional business credits or experience.
EDUCATION: Required is a high school diploma plus a bachelor's degree in engineering or other related scientific field.
EXPERIENCE: Some experience in scientific or engineering is usually necessary.
PERSONALITY: One must be logical, intelligent, and methodical.
ENVIRONMENT: A scientific programmer works on a computer terminal in a professional office setting, with occasional time in the laboratory or plant.
TRAVEL: Minimal, except for trade shows, seminars, and schooling.
SALARY: The range is $18,000 to $30,000, depending primarily on experience, but also on company size and location.
INSIDE INFORMATION: This is not a very competitive position; plenty of job opportunities exist. Since the work involves programming of the highest caliber, there is some intellectual status associated with it. The scientific programmer also enjoys working in a structured environment, adhering to specific rules and conditions laid down for the project. But he can be under stress due to the need for intense concentration on the job and because he works alone most of the time. This position is usually found in large software companies.

CONTRACT PROGRAMMER

A contract programmer is like a consultant: his services are freelanced to hardware or software companies needing his service or specialization. Most of his time is spent designing, writing, and documenting programs under the direction of the client's project leader. He also codes, draws charts, and writes instructions.

This position requires an individual well suited to travel, being away from home, and adjusting to living in a city for weeks or months at a time. He also must be able to get along with people even though much of the actual work is done alone.
RELATED TITLE: None.
ADVANCEMENT: This position is limited in the sense that it is not on the corporate ladder. Like the consultant, the contract programmer may be his own boss or may work for a consulting firm that markets contract programmers.
EDUCATION: A bachelor's degree in computer science or a related field is necessary.
EXPERIENCE: Two or more years in programming is the minimum one would need.
PERSONALITY: This person must be able to deal with different kinds of people, yet maintain a level of exceptional achievement.

ENVIRONMENT: The setting is the client's office, with perhaps lower quality accommodations than desired.
TRAVEL: Considerable movement between clients, as most of the work is done at the customer's site.
SALARY: The range is from $18,000 to $30,000 and higher, depending on the contract programmer's experience, reputation, specialty (if any), and current demand.
INSIDE INFORMATION: Pressures include close scrutiny and checking of work by the client, as well as deadlines. This person needs to be strong and somewhat aggressive, since demands made of him are usually more than those made of ordinary programmers.

COMMUNICATIONS PROGRAMMER

The communications programmer works with the design and testing of network software—that is, information available to a network of computer users tied into a central operations center. Networking actually involves the marriage of two sciences—computers and communications, since networks involve multiple computers, terminals, and other equipment (satellites, microwave devices) that are tied together by telephone lines to create a complete communications environment. Programmers must learn *both* of these sciences to some degree.

The job includes the actual writing and testing of the program(s). This challenging spot carries with it the thrill of being involved in the leading edge of technology. Though the programmer works alone much of the time, the end result of his efforts involves hundreds or thousands of people using a communication programmer's system at any one time.
RELATED TITLES: Senior or junior communications programmer.
ADVANCEMENT: Progression is limited to technical areas in the area of network analysis.
EDUCATION: A bachelor's degree in computer science with credits in communications and network theory is needed.
EXPERIENCE: Two years as an applications programmer or support/maintenance programmer with additional experience in assembly language helpful.
PERSONALITY: A very logical and thorough person functions best in this position.
ENVIRONMENT: One can expect odd hours in the computer room and office setting.
TRAVEL: About 10 percent of the time.
SALARY: $18,000 to $30,000 depending on the size of the company, location, and experience.
INSIDE INFORMATION: Because of the current explosion in the area of

electronic communications and networking, this area will probably be both popular and competitive in the years to come. With this in mind it would be smart to combine the basics of communications programming with additional education in general management.

DATA-BASE PROGRAMMER

The person in this position is concerned with the development, design, and testing of a data-base structure, which is a base of information (such as employee data) that various end-users can gain access to for information. Most of his time is spent in developing the actual program, with some time spent in chart drawing, preparing layouts, and coding.

Found usually in large software firms, this is a basic position; with additional education the programmer can advance.

RELATED TITLES: Senior, junior, or assistant data-base programmer.
ADVANCEMENT: This position leads directly to data-base analyst and, with proper experience, to data administrator.
EDUCATION: A bachelor's degree in computer science with credits in data-base technology is the requirement. Specialty training in data-base programming would be a significant plus.
EXPERIENCE: Three or more years in applications or systems programming is the norm.
PERSONALITY: A technically oriented, logical person is good for this spot.
ENVIRONMENT: The office is the primary setting.
TRAVEL: Minimal.
SALARY: $20,000 to $30,000, depending on company size, location, and programmer's experience.
INSIDE INFORMATION: This is a steady-paced, limited-pressure position, not involving much at-home work. Since the pay is good, it is competitive, and opportunities have to be found. The programmer works alone much of the time, but usually finds his work personally satisfying.

NETWORK ANALYST

This person designs and builds networks—systems that allow for transfer of information and communications between many people—for end-user access. He must know how to specify and purchase equipment for the project. Additionally, his duties involve hands-on programming, network setup, testing, and operating, as well as some supervision of analysts and programmers.

This position, found usually in large firms both in the software and hardware areas, will have future potential as the field begins to open up.

RELATED TITLES: None.

ADVANCEMENT: This type of work is limited usually to technical careers. With additional credits, one can advance into management.

EDUCATION: A bachelor's degree in computer science with advanced credits in communications and network theory is required. Other credits in areas such as microwave communications and message switching are helpful.

EXPERIENCE: Three or more years as a programmer and two as a communications programmer are a solid background.

PERSONALITY: This person must be very logical and good at details.

ENVIRONMENT: The office is the setting.

TRAVEL: Roughly 10 percent of the time.

SALARY: The range is from $20,000 to $35,000, depending mainly on experience, but also on company size and location.

INSIDE INFORMATION: Due to the advanced technical nature of this position, the network analyst must keep up with the latest technology. His job often necessitates at-home work, as well as working closely with people in many different areas. He is under both day-to-day deadline pressure and mental strain, but the rewards of status, power, and control seem to outweigh the drawbacks of the long work hours required. The competition is keen, as the pay and career possibilities are good.

SYSTEMS ANALYST

The person in this position is heavily involved with the design of a system to solve, usually, business-related problems concerned with the flow of information. Some programming is required from time to time; the writing of documentation is also required, as are presentations to clients, training of end-users, and program coding. Additionally, there may be some supervision of coworkers.

Found in both large software and hardware firms, the position of systems analyst is competitive: not only is the pay good but there is much satisfaction to be gained.

RELATED TITLES: Systems designer, systems engineer (senior, chief, principal).

ADVANCEMENT: This position can lead to project management and possible corporate management posts.

EDUCATION: You need a bachelor's degree in computer science or related area. An MBA or advanced degree in computer science is very helpful.

EXPERIENCE: Three years in programming are necessary; several years in a business area are a plus.
PERSONALITY: One must be organized, methodical, and intelligent to be a good systems analyst.
ENVIRONMENT: Though there are some meetings, most of the work is in an office setting.
TRAVEL: Occasional, for committee meetings or seminars.
SALARY: The range is $20,000 to $35,000, depending on company size and experience.
INSIDE INFORMATION: The systems analyst works with many people in designing his system, and enjoys the intellectual status and benefits that come from being a leader. This person is also visible in the corporate structure and there are many advancement opportunities for the person who keeps his eyes and ears open.

CHIEF PROGRAMMER

This is a high-level post involving the overseeing of team(s) of programmers assigned to develop part of a large project or a single small project. The chief programmer is also directly involved in design and programming work on the team, as well as coding, documentation, and training.

This position is found mainly in large hardware and software firms, and offers the person in it status and visibility within the corporation. Financial rewards and increased responsibilities are accompanied by mental stress and deadline pressures.
RELATED TITLES: None.
ADVANCEMENT: This is a highly visible post, and with proper training can lead to project manager.
EDUCATION: A bachelor's degree in computer science or a related field is necessary.
EXPERIENCE: A total of five or more years split between systems design and programming is desirable.
PERSONALITY: An aggressive, intelligent person who is able to lead small groups of people effectively is ideal for this position.
ENVIRONMENT: The professional office is the setting, with work performed on a computer terminal.
TRAVEL: Scattered, for meetings, training, or seminars.
SALARY: From $25,000 to $35,000, depending on personal experience, company and department size, and location.
INSIDE INFORMATION: As this is a position with good advancement possibilities, the competition is keen. An individual here must be able to define work areas and utilize creative approaches to problems. He also needs to communicate well with people on all levels in the firm.

DATA-BASE ADMINISTRATOR

This person is responsible for the design, creation, and operation of new data bases (banks of information) for corporate business areas. The data-base administrator usually heads up a group of several analysts and programmers who oversee this data-base function. Correspondence, chart drawing, and writing specifications are also part of this job.

This is another plum position, offering high visibility, advancement potential, and a commensurate salary. Of course, this is not without the daily deadlines and mental strains found in any position managing people and projects. The position is also highly competitive.

RELATED TITLES: None.

ADVANCEMENT: This position has good exposure to other parts of the company and, with proper experience, can lead to departmental and company management posts.

EDUCATION: An MBA would be a big plus to go along with a bachelor's degree in computer science.

EXPERIENCE: Five to six years, split between systems design/analysis and programming, with an emphasis on data base programming.

PERSONALITY: Management skills are necessary, along with the ability to lead and motivate people.

ENVIRONMENT: There is considerable involvement in meetings and with customers in various office settings.

TRAVEL: About 10 percent of the time, for committee meetings, seminars, and contact with clients.

SALARY: $25,000 to $35,000, depending on the data-base department's size.

INSIDE INFORMATION: This person will enjoy traveling as well as being part of the political "inside" of the corporation. The data-base administrator is in a unique position. He must fill specific requests—all of which are needed "yesterday"—from almost every department in the firm. In order to do so he must be good at bargaining, negotiation, and compromise.

PROJECT MANAGER

This position involves the direction of people who form project teams—numbering up to thirty people each. A specific project's outcome is the responsibility of this person, and continued successes will be noticed. Additional work includes technical involvement, writing, preparing presentations and documentation.

This typical managerial position brings with it day-to-day deadlines associated with the project's requirements, along with rewards such as enjoyable travel, power, and political involvement within the company.

RELATED TITLES: Project director, project leader.
ADVANCEMENT: This position has high corporate visibility and can lead to other management posts.
EDUCATION: A bachelor's degree in computer science is necessary, and an MBA or equivalent experience is strongly advised.
EXPERIENCE: Five to six years are necessary in these areas: systems design/analysis, programming or business.
PERSONALITY: An even-tempered person who can effectively lead people is desired. The project manager must be technically competent.
ENVIRONMENT: There is much interaction in the office setting, including meetings and phone conversations.
TRAVEL: About one-fifth of the time, for committee meetings, customer contact, and for contract work.
SALARY: Project managers earn from $25,000 to $40,000 and higher, depending on personal experience and successes and company size.
INSIDE INFORMATION: This position requires working closely with other coworkers, customers, and subordinates to make an effective project. Found in the hardware and software sectors of both large and small firms, a project manager is always "on the spot," with people ready to move in should he falter. Few opportunities exist here as it is a solid and highly competitive management position. Much work is done after hours.

MANAGER—SYSTEMS DEVELOPMENT

This person works with and directs other development project managers. A broad technical knowledge base enables the systems development manager to assist managers working on a variety of projects.

This is a top-notch position in the development area, requiring an individual who works well with people within the firm and with the firm's customers. He is not only responsible for many projects but must develop a rapport with his managers. In the fast-paced, constantly changing environment that characterizes this position, the system development manager must really be "on the ball."
RELATED TITLES: Director—project development.
ADVANCEMENT: This is another highly visible post that can lead to other management positions.
EDUCATION: A bachelor's degree in computer science and an MBA or equivalent advanced degree (or experience) are mandatory for this post.
EXPERIENCE: Over five years is necessary in these areas: systems design/analysis, project leadership, the technical area (programming, operations, etc.), and the business area.

PERSONALITY: This spot requires poise, the ability to take control under pressure, and the ability to deal effectively with people in large groups and in one-on-one situations. Good written and oral communications skills are also required.
ENVIRONMENT: The office is the central point for meetings and interaction with people.
TRAVEL: About 20 percent, for committee meetings, customer contact, and contract work.
SALARY: A broad range from $30,000 to $50,000, depending on size of company, personal experience, and location.
INSIDE INFORMATION: This person is a good manager of people, knowing when to use his power, control, and political influence. He copes easily with stresses from different areas and can switch from one project to another during the day when problems arise. This spot is found in large and small hardware and software firms. Considerable after-hours work/thought is required.

CONSULTANT

The consultant designs systems and programs for customers who choose to utilize an outside freelancer. Occasionally he supervises other programmers and prepares written materials and charts.

In addition to being technically proficient and good at his computer work, a consultant also has to know how to run his business, which carries with it additional pressures. His added responsibilities include bookkeeping, advertising and promotion, billing, and collections. While the personal satisfaction, financial rewards, and the pleasure from "being your own boss" can be high, a lot must be sacrificed to get them.
RELATED TITLES: None.
ADVANCEMENT: This job is not under the corporate umbrella; the consultant is usually self-employed, with the corresponding advantages and disadvantages. A consultant's business can grow with the hiring of staff to work for him.
EDUCATION: To become a top consultant, you need a BS in computer science or related field, an MBA or other advanced degree, and specialty courses in various areas of data processing.
EXPERIENCE: Seven to nine years of systems and programming work is the norm.
PERSONALITY: A good communicator (oral and written) who is fairly aggressive will do well in this career.
ENVIRONMENT: Usually at the customer's site. Accommodations may be less than pleasing.

TRAVEL: Consistent travel and relocation from job site to job site.
SALARY: Consultants earn from $25,000 to $45,000 and up, depending on experience and area of expertise.
INSIDE INFORMATION: A consultant will have plenty of paid overtime opportunities, usually away from home. This job reflects many of the ups and downs associated with the economy or the success/failure of the company he is working for. A very stable person able to handle all kinds of pressure is needed here.

THE MAINTENANCE AREA

SUPPORT PROGRAMMER

This person reviews, corrects, and updates existing programs, including coding changes and the rewriting of instructions. He usually has no supervisory responsibilities, and has plenty of paid overtime opportunity to compensate for deadline pressures. Much of his work is done by himself.
RELATED TITLES: Maintenance programmer.
ADVANCEMENT: With proper training and experience, one can move into application or systems programming.
EDUCATION: A high school diploma with credits in computer science or an associate degree is preferred.
EXPERIENCE: This is an entry-level position.
PERSONALITY: Logical and detail-oriented.
ENVIRONMENT: Work is performed on a terminal in an office.
TRAVEL: None, except perhaps for training.
SALARY: From $12,000 to $20,000, depending on company size and current needs.
INSIDE INFORMATION: This position is well defined whether it's found in software or hardware firms (usually large ones). Since the hours are long and the pay average, many job opportunities exist. The job is a challenge that can provide a feeling of intellectual accomplishment. By no means is it a dead end.

SYSTEMS PROGRAMMER

While a support programmer usually *fixes* old programs, systems programmers usually *write* new ones.
The function of this position is to write, test, and document programs dealing with operating systems or related software. This includes coding, chart drawing, and other support activities.

Design and Manufacturing

A person here will find plenty of work, most of it done alone.
RELATED TITLES: Senior, junior, or assistant systems programmer.
ADVANCEMENT: Limited to progress in the specialty areas of systems programming. Additional, broader-based education is needed for advancement into other areas.
EDUCATION: A bachelor's degree in computer science with specialty training in assembly language, compiler design, and operating systems is necessary.
EXPERIENCE: Two or more years in applications programming; this is normally not an entry-level job.
PERSONALITY: Highly technically oriented.
ENVIRONMENT: Time is split between the office and computer room; work is done on a terminal.
TRAVEL: Minimal.
SALARY: From $15,000 to $30,000, depending on the company's requirements, needs, and location.
INSIDE INFORMATION: This position is appealing because it is intellectually involving and therefore personally satisfying. Also, while in this position a person can take advantage of the many options open in a large hardware or software firm. Exciting, dynamic, fast-paced, and ever-changing, this job is a real challenge for the "with it" person.

SUPPORT ANALYST

The support analyst is usually responsible for overseeing projects such as generating new systems, installing new releases of software, and program coding, charting, and writing. Since the area of software is quite specialized, the position of support analyst is a specialized title too.

This position offers good pay, bonuses, and a high level of personal satisfaction related to intellectual achievement. Duties may include some supervision of workers, depending on the company.
RELATED TITLES: Senior, junior, or assistant support analyst.
ADVANCEMENT: Limited to the systems programming or support areas, because of the high degree of specialization. It is difficult to advance without further training and experience, more general in nature.
EDUCATION: A BS in computer science with additional training in operating systems, compiler design, and assembly languages is required.
EXPERIENCE: Four to five years, split between application programming and design.
PERSONALITY: This person must be highly technically oriented and also a good problem solver or troubleshooter.

ENVIRONMENT: The work is performed in either the computer room or office.
TRAVEL: Minimal.
SALARY: $20,000 to $35,000, depending on experience level and company size.
INSIDE INFORMATION: Many job opportunities exist in this area, which is characterized by a fast pace and constantly changing technological environment. While there are sometimes large amounts of after-hours work, the personal satisfaction obtained from it is high.

MANAGER—SUPPORT

This supervisor usually oversees small department(s) of systems programmers, a job requiring good managerial skills as well as the ability to handle the pressures associated with managing projects and people. He is involved heavily with day-to-day assignments on a highly technical level.

This is a highly visible spot within the corporation, with plenty of responsibility. The pressure to produce is rewarded by good pay, power, and an entry into the political fabric of the corporation.
RELATED TITLES: Manager (Director) of systems programming.
ADVANCEMENT: Advancement is limited to management posts within computer areas. Corporate areas can be reached with additional experience, exposure, or education.
EDUCATION: A bachelor's degree in computer science with advanced training in operating system theory, internals, and compiler design is required.
EXPERIENCE: Five to six years in programming using assembly or machine languages are needed.
ENVIRONMENT: The office is the main setting, with some work in the computer operations areas on terminals.
TRAVEL: Minimal.
SALARY: $25,000 to $40,000, depending on company and department size as well as personal experience.
INSIDE INFORMATION: Both the pace and competition are in the fast lane, so a person thinking of support management needs to be able to think quickly and creatively. Extra work is completed after hours or at home.

THE PRODUCTION AREA

Production career summaries can be found in Chapter 8, "Word and Data Processing." These careers are available in both hardware

Design and Manufacturing

and software companies, so someone considering software as a profession should not overlook this set of jobs.

THE TRAINING AREA

The three positions in this area, outlined under hardware, are available in software companies as well.

7. SERVICE, MAINTENANCE, AND INSTALLATION

While most personal computers rarely need to be serviced as they can be purchased, taken home, and plugged right into a wall outlet, this is not the case with larger systems. In fact, the area of servicing computers is one of the fastest-growing segments of the entire computer industry! Because machines do break down for a variety of reasons, technically competent service personnel must always be available to keep "down time" at a minimum.

In addition, larger systems must be installed at a customer's site, which takes considerably more effort than plugging a wire into an outlet. On-site servicing is an excellent area for someone with good manual dexterity and a flair for troubleshooting and solving problems.

Service is provided both by independent service and maintenance firms and by hardware and software companies. When applying for any of the positions listed below, remember that you have these two areas—independent companies and divisions of larger firms—to look into.

SERVICE, MAINTENANCE AND INSTALLATION CAREER SUMMARIES

TECHNICIAN

The technician spends about 70 percent of his time servicing and fixing computers. He provides both routine preventive maintenance and troubleshooting to solve specific problems. The other 30 percent of his time is spent learning and reviewing the maintenance, repair, and installation procedures for various equipment lines serviced, which is information found in manuals published by equipment manufacturers.

This job is an excellent opportunity for someone who enjoys a challenge combining physical, manual, and mental skills. He should enjoy working alone at a variety of locations as he services different clients.

RELATED TITLES: Senior or assistant technician.
ADVANCEMENT: Without additional training or college credits, advancement is difficult. After working as a technician, one can become a technical specialist, field engineer or service manager.
EDUCATION: A high school diploma, an associate degree, or trade school education in computer repair and maintenance is required.
EXPERIENCE: This is an entry-level position requiring no previous experience.
PERSONALITY: One should be logical, alert, and mechanically inclined. Having a "sixth sense" about what's wrong is a most desirable trait.
ENVIRONMENT: The technician works in customer sites wherever the computers are located.
TRAVEL: Most of the time is spent traveling between repair and maintenance jobs. Travel may be local or interstate depending on the size of the company and the service department.
SALARY: Technicians earn from $10,000 to $20,000. Top-notch repair people can eventually open their own independent repair services.
INSIDE INFORMATION: Many job opportunities exist in this area, and paid overtime is widely available. Pressures are both mental and physical; a person with the "knack" for solving problems does well here. Personal satisfaction is gained from knowing that whole departments producing millions of documents depend on your finding and fixing the trouble.

TECHNICAL SPECIALIST

This person is actually a technician who has developed or been assigned a specialty on certain types of equipment, by either brand of machine or type of machine. He must understand everything there is to know about his specialty in order to profitably spend time servicing, troubleshooting, and repairing computer systems.

This position is found mainly in large hardware and software companies and in independent service firms. Because of the specialized nature of the work, this position provides both personal enrichment and intellectual status.

RELATED TITLES: Senior or junior technical specialist.
ADVANCEMENT: Can lead to field engineering and service management with additional training or experience.
EDUCATION: A high school diploma plus an associate degree or other technical training in computer service is required.
EXPERIENCE: Two years as a technician should be satisfactory for this position.
PERSONALITY: The technical specialist should be logical, thorough, and like to work with his hands in solving problems.

ENVIRONMENT: The computer room of the various customer sites is where the service work is performed.
TRAVEL: Most of the time depending on where the clients are located.
SALARY: $15,000 to $25,000.
INSIDE INFORMATION: As the specialist's knowledge becomes more and more refined and he gains a reputation, opportunities increase. There always seems to be something new to learn as new models of the same basic machine come out. A good understanding of technical manuals and schematic diagrams is a major requirement for this position.

FIELD ENGINEER

The major task of the field engineer is the installation of new systems. He first analyzes the customer's site and then works with the company in laying out the room(s) and installing climate-control devices and electrical wiring. He also helps with the delivery of the hardware and sets up the system so it runs without problems. Additional people often help the field engineer with this initial setup and "hand-holding" of the customer's employees in the first introductory weeks.

This is a position for a leader who enjoys the final stages of a project: setup, testing, training, and getting the system "on-line" (ready to go).

RELATED TITLES: Senior or junior field engineer, service engineer, customer engineer.
ADVANCEMENT: With additional credits and experience, one can advance to management positions.
EDUCATION: Required is a high school diploma along with an associate degree or equivalent technical training in computer servicing.
EXPERIENCE: Several years as a technician or technical specialist are preferred.
PERSONALITY: In addition to being alert and observant, this person should be thorough, logical, and able to get along with people.
ENVIRONMENT: The computer rooms of the firm's customers are the environment.
TRAVEL: Much of the time is spent traveling from job site to job site; sometimes it is necessary to visit several sites in one day.
SALARY: $20,000 to $35,000, depending on the field engineer's experience and expertise.
INSIDE INFORMATION: As is true with most service and installation positions, coping with urgent deadlines, constant travel and changing customer sites can produce both physical and mental pressures. However, extra monies can be earned through paid overtime. Job opportunities exist in most firms, but competition is growing as people

recognize the need for competent field engineers and other service personnel.

SERVICE MANAGER

The service manager oversees the staff of service and installation specialists. His responsibilities include scheduling, problem-solving, hiring, and keeping abreast of the latest equipment and service procedures. He may be called in on tough assignments or seemingly insoluable problems.

This is more of a management position than one of direct service, and it requires a person good at handling people, scheduling assignments, and keeping everyone happy. As the amount of down time reflects on a company's product, this position is highly visible: quick solutions bring "thank you's" from customers to management.

RELATED TITLES: None.
ADVANCEMENT: This position can lead to other corporate management positions with additional education and experience in other areas.
EDUCATION: A bachelor's degree in computer science or in another area with sufficient technical courses is appropriate.
EXPERIENCE: A total of four to five years split between being a technician or technical specialist and a field engineer, is the right background.
PERSONALITY: This person must be a good coordinator, organizer, and administrator, in addition to being technically sharp and up to date.
ENVIRONMENT: The office is the primary setting.
TRAVEL: Perhaps 10 percent of the time, to customer sites.
SALARY: A broad range from $20,000 to $40,000, depending on the size of the service department and the range of the territory covered.
INSIDE INFORMATION: Good service and installation people compete for this position, and for that reason opportunities aren't as plentiful as for the other service spots. Additionally, the service manager must be a generalist familiar with many machines, because the final responsibility for repair rests with him. This creates additional pressures.

8. WORD AND DATA PROCESSING

This area of computing is the largest in terms of number of employees. Word and data processing personnel are employed by all the end-users of computers, both in the private sector and in government. As more and more organizations—whether small law firms or giant corporations—buy computing systems, the word/data processing career area becomes increasingly important.

As a whole, this group of people takes raw data, inputs the data into the computer, processes it by updating, sorting and printing it, produces records, and then uses this information to help businesses perform better. Job titles are split into two sections: data processing and word processing. There is a little overlapping, but for the most part the functions are different.

In most cases data processing people work with numbers, names, and addresses; some of the services provided through data processing include producing mailing labels, sending out bills, and keeping records. Word processing people, on the other hand, handle documents such as letters, reports, and other correspondence.

As with the chapter on design and manufacturing, we will indicate which careers are found primarily in either the hardware or software areas and also mention those found in both.

DATA-PROCESSING CAREER SUMMARIES

LIBRARIAN

The librarian is responsible for keeping track of all the magnetic media such as disks, tapes, and forms used in the data-processing operation and may also use a computer terminal for job setup, tape pulling, and scheduling. He enjoys the security of a nine-to-five, steadily paced job in which the main responsibility is locating materials efficiently and quickly. There is little pressure—except, of course, when materials seem to be missing.
RELATED TITLES: Senior or junior librarian.
ADVANCEMENT: Without additional training, advancement is limited to senior librarian or other data-control positions.
EDUCATION: A high school diploma is all that is required; computer courses are an added plus.

EXPERIENCE: This is an entry-level spot.
PERSONALITY: This person should be organized and thorough.
ENVIRONMENT: The work takes place in the computer operations area, usually in or near the computer room.
TRAVEL: None.
SALARY: $8,000 to $15,000, depending on the size of the library.
INSIDE INFORMATION: This position is found either in a hardware or software firm. It is very structured, with many guidelines provided for procedures, and involves much working alone and searching out the correct materials.

JOB-CONTROL CLERK

The job-control clerk is responsible for processing work orders and preparing the accounting (numbers, times, costs, etc.) for jobs scheduled for processing. He handles and delivers printouts upon completion, and must make sure that the information required is what is on the final printout, labels or reports.

Another basic position, this is found in large and small software and hardware firms, and offers both security and little pressure for the individual who doesn't mind working alone for much of the time.
RELATED TITLES: Data-control clerk, senior or junior job-control clerk.
ADVANCEMENT: Without training in a specialty area such as operations or programming, the job is limited to the control positions.
EDUCATION: A high school diploma is necessary, and additional computer training is desirable.
EXPERIENCE: This is an entry-level job.
PERSONALITY: This person should be well organized and able to easily follow directions.
ENVIRONMENT: The work area is the input/output area, usually a "bull pen" arrangement of workers.
TRAVEL: None.
SALARY: $8,000 to $15,000, depending on company and department size, location, and experience.
INSIDE INFORMATION: Plenty of job opportunities exist as there isn't much competition for these jobs. They are routine and mechanical, with little responsibility. The ideal worker here will enjoy working within established guidelines and following set procedures.

TAB-EQUIPMENT OPERATOR

The tab-equipment operator operates various types of machines that process computer cards, forms, and tapes by reading data, processing it, and then printing the desired information onto computer forms.

There is minimal technical knowledge required and no supervisory responsibilities.

Like the previous two jobs described, this position is good for a person who wants a steady pace and income without being hassled by pressures typically associated with management positions.

RELATED TITLES: Senior or junior tab-equipment operator.
ADVANCEMENT: Progression is limited without training in a specialty such as operations or programming.
EDUCATION: A high school diploma is required.
EXPERIENCE: This is an entry-level post.
PERSONALITY: A thorough and steady person is good for this job.
ENVIRONMENT: This person uses bursting machines (which separate computer paper sheets), decollators, sorters, tape/disk cleaners, printers, and other devices in the computer room area.
TRAVEL: None.
SALARY: $8,000 to $15,000, depending on company size, workload, and location.
INSIDE INFORMATION: The competition for this job is not tough, whether the candidate is looking in large or small hardware or software firms. There is a degree of personal satisfaction in being a competent operator with a reputation for making few errors.

CRT OPERATOR

A CRT (cathode ray tube) operator uses a keyboard to input data into a computer system on the terminal screen. Most of his time is involved in this area; this is a heavy input position, since raw data must be gotten into the system for processing. Some light data-processing activities may also be involved.

There's never a problem with opportunity here, since firms need manpower to input data. This is a good position for the eight-hour-day-oriented person who likes manual typing and doesn't mind working alone at the keyboard.

RELATED TITLES: Senior or junior CRT operator.
ADVANCEMENT: Limited to supervisory position in this area without additional training or experience.
EDUCATION: A high school diploma with typing or other keyboard training is required.
EXPERIENCE: This is an entry-level position.
PERSONALITY: Accuracy and steadiness are important.
ENVIRONMENT: All the work takes place in the computer operations area, similar to an open computer room.
TRAVEL: None.
SALARY: $8,000 to $18,000, depending on experience, company size, and location.

Word and Data Processing

INSIDE INFORMATION: Here you'll find little job competition, whether in large or small or hardware or software firms. There isn't much mental strain attached to this position, but sitting in front of the screen and typing for long periods of time can cause physical pressure.

KEY-TAPE OPERATOR

The key-tape operator inputs data into key-tape machines, which are devices that transcribe typed data onto magnetic tape. There is no technical knowledge or supervisory ability required for this position.

This is another of the secure data-input positions requiring a person who enjoys steady work, good compensation, and little pressure.

RELATED TITLES: Senior or junior key-tape operator.
ADVANCEMENT: Progress is limited to supervisor in this area. Advancement beyond that post is available with additional training and experience.
EDUCATION: A high school diploma with typing or other keyboard training, preferably on key-tape machines, is preferred.
EXPERIENCE: This is an entry-level position.
PERSONALITY: Thoroughness, patience, and accuracy.
ENVIRONMENT: The computer operations area—an open computer room—is the setting.
TRAVEL: None.
SALARY: $8,000 to $18,000, depending on workload, experience, and company size.
INSIDE INFORMATION: Plenty of opportunities exist for this position (as is true of other data entry positions) in large hardware or software companies. The guidelines and procedures are straightforward; the average workday is eight hours; and there is no need to bring work home or endure some of the stresses and problems management faces.

KEYPUNCH OPERATOR

A keypunch operator works on keypunch machines, inputting data which is converted into punched holes on computer cards. Occasionally this person may have to set up or format "program cards," which are used in the keypunch machines.

While this position can be found in large or small software or hardware firms, the opportunities are limited, as described below.

RELATED TITLES: Senior or junior keypunch operator.
ADVANCEMENT: Progress is limited to supervisory positions in this area. Other advancement is possible with additional training and experience.
EDUCATION: One would need a high school diploma, with training in typing or keypunching.

EXPERIENCE: This is an entry-level position.
PERSONALITY: One should be thorough, steady, and accurate.
ENVIRONMENT: The work is performed in the computer operations area.
TRAVEL: None.
SALARY: The range is $8,000 to $18,000, depending on company size, location, and personal experience.
INSIDE INFORMATION: Even though there are hundreds of thousands of keypunch operators, I would not recommend this as a promising field for the future. With the increasing popularity of cathode ray tubes, keypunching with cards is on the decline; new operators are hired only to make up for losses caused by attrition. Companies heavily invested in keypunching will remain with it (as opposed to CRT data entry), but the future is limited. If this doesn't make a difference to you, you might find what you're looking for here.

AUXILIARY EQUIPMENT OPERATOR

This person does exactly what the title implies: he operates various types of equipment associated with the central computer, such as tape drives, disk drives, and printers. There are no technical or supervisory responsibilities. In addition to working the machines, he clears mechanical problems such as paper jams or bad tapes.

Found primarily in large or small hardware firms, this position is well defined and structured with steady hours.
RELATED TITLES: None.
ADVANCEMENT: Limited, though one can progress to computer operator. Other positions require additional training or experience.
EDUCATION: A high school diploma is all that's necessary.
EXPERIENCE: This is an entry-level position.
PERSONALITY: One should be alert and thorough.
ENVIRONMENT: The computer room, a large open area, is the setting.
TRAVEL: None.
SALARY: $10,000 to $20,000, depending on company size, location, and personal experience.
INSIDE INFORMATION: As more and more firms buy equipment, more opportunities will exist for operators of both computers and their related devices.

COMPUTER OPERATOR

The computer operator operates the computer console, printers, tape drives, and other peripheral equipment. He is responsible for setup, execution, and completion of all jobs on assigned machines.

Word and Data Processing

The console operator runs the whole system—not just a part of it (as the auxiliary equipment operator does)—and directs others who work individual machines. Some time is spent learning about new systems, and there may be some supervision of clerks or auxiliary operators.

This position carries more responsibility and pressure than those covered so far in this area. Some of the work is physical; the computer operator may have to lift paper and other supplies, which sometimes may be heavy.

RELATED TITLES: Senior or lead computer operator.
ADVANCEMENT: With additional credits and/or experience this position can lead to shift supervisor and other operations management posts.
EDUCATION: A high school degree and an associate degree or technical training as an operator are required.
EXPERIENCE: This is an entry-level position, which occasionally may require experience as a control clerk or auxiliary equipment operator.
PERSONALITY: This person must be alert and able to handle several tasks at the same time.
ENVIRONMENT: The computer room, where there can be considerable noise, is the setting.
TRAVEL: Minimal.
SALARY: $12,000 to $20,000, depending on experience, company size, and departmental workload.
INSIDE INFORMATION: The person in this spot enjoys having his time split between working alone and with others; he also has a degree of intellectual status as his work is more than mechanical. Opportunities are plentiful in both large and small hardware firms, but there is competition for these jobs. The work is dynamic and fast-paced.

NETWORK OPERATOR

In a large, communications-oriented company or installation, the network operator is responsible for servicing and operating the equipment that is tied into the main computer. In many cases, smaller computers are used. The network operator must understand the technical aspects of communications networks and the sophisticated equipment involved.

This is a very interesting position because of the recent rapid development of communications networks. However, the pressures that arise from daily deadlines are a constant here. A problem in the main computer can affect hundreds or thousands of terminals tied into it and must be corrected quickly.

RELATED TITLES: None.

ADVANCEMENT: Progress is limited to the operations area. With a college degree or advanced training, other areas are accessible.
EDUCATION: A high school diploma with training in communications and network control is required.
EXPERIENCE: Some time as a computer operator and/or technician is helpful.
PERSONALITY: This person should be alert and a fast thinker.
ENVIRONMENT: This job is performed in the computer room area.
TRAVEL: Minimal.
SALARY: $12,000 to $20,000, depending on experience, company size, and departmental workload.
INSIDE INFORMATION: Few opportunities exist here, and for that reason, the competition is keen. It's a position that requires both a commitment to a specialty right from the start and the desire to work in a large firm.

COMMUNICATIONS SPECIALIST

The communications specialist is responsible for overseeing the operation and maintenance of the communication equipment (telephone switches, modems, etc.) connected to the computer terminals and consoles in a company specializing in communications or the communications department of a large hardware or software company. The work is roughly split in half between the actual manual operation (running the machines) and keeping up with new technology. Personal satisfaction can be gained from learning the complicated equipment and operating procedures involved here.
RELATED TITLES: None.
ADVANCEMENT: Moving ahead is limited without additional credits, training, or experience.
EDUCATION: A high school diploma and an associate degree in communication/electronics are necessary.
EXPERIENCE: Several years as a technician is the norm for this post.
PERSONALITY: One should have good technical ability and be a logical and detail-oriented person.
ENVIRONMENT: The computer room and/or communications area is the setting.
TRAVEL: None.
SALARY: $15,000 to $25,000, depending on experience, size of department or company, and location.
INSIDE INFORMATION: Personal satisfaction can be gained from learning the complicated equipment and operating procedures involved here. However, due to the highly technical nature of this position, the fact that much of the work is done alone, and the need for long hours and at-home work, mental pressure can accompany this job.

The opportunities beyond this position require a broader perspective; since the area of communications is increasing in popularity, further education should be considered.

JOB-CONTROL SUPERVISOR

This job involves three distinct areas of responsibility: overseeing or supervising a group of job-control clerks; maintaining a good working knowledge of the various equipment and procedures used; and some operation of the computer input machines during heavy load periods or personnel shortages.

The job-control supervisor should be a management-oriented person who enjoys working with machines and people to produce the required work efficiently. He will be involved with others, including management; a good reputation as a job-control supervisor can lead to bigger and better positions.

RELATED TITLES: None.
ADVANCEMENT: Basically limited to shift supervisor. With additional college training, higher titles are accessible.
EDUCATION: A high school diploma and an associate degree or similar training are required.
EXPERIENCE: Two to four years as a computer operator is necessary.
PERSONALITY: Technical thoroughness and the ability to lead personnel effectively are required.
ENVIRONMENT: The work site is the computer operations area.
TRAVEL: None.
SALARY: From $15,000 to $25,000, depending on experience, size of department, and location.
INSIDE INFORMATION: Supervisory positions are always competitive, and this one is no exception, whether it is in a large or small software-oriented firm. Day-to-day deadlines can create pressure, but a degree of personal satisfaction and the feeling of "being noticed" by higher-ups are good compensations. A good performer here can advance further, as indicated above.

KEYPUNCH SUPERVISOR

Several keypunch operators work under a keypunch supervisor, whose job is to keep all keypunching operations and equipment running at optimum efficiency. There may be some hands-on operation during heavy-load periods or during personnel shortages or vacations.

This position has some elements of management since the supervisor must take charge of people and report to others instead of working alone. It's basically a nine-to-five job that can be found in both large and small software firms.

RELATED TITLES: None.
ADVANCEMENT: Shift supervisor is the title after keypunch supervisor. Higher positions can be attained only with additional college training.
EDUCATION: Required are a high school diploma and an associate degree or similar vocational training.
EXPERIENCE: Two to four years as a general operator is sufficient.
PERSONALITY: This person should be even-tempered, able to get along well with people, and sharp.
ENVIRONMENT: The keypunch supervisor's work area is the keypunch room.
TRAVEL: None.
SALARY: $15,000 to $25,000, depending on experience, size of department, and location.
INSIDE INFORMATION: Because this position involves managing people and machines in order to meet daily deadlines, there are accompanying mental and physical pressures. On the positive side, power and good pay go along with this position. However, since the number of keypunch operators is decreasing (see keypunch operator summary), the future of keypunch supervisors does not seem bright. Approach this position cautiously should you have higher ambitions.

SHIFT SUPERVISOR

Found primarily in hardware firms, the shift supervisor oversees all of the computer operators and auxiliary operators for a single department or installation (one company or site where a computer system is installed). The job involves many different kinds of machines about which the shift supervisor (several of whom work in shifts) must be technically knowledgeable. During personnel shortages the supervisor may be involved in actual operation.

As with other management positions, power and visibility are part of the job. Due to the responsibilities inherent here, both the rewards (financial, status, etc.) and pressures (managing people, machines and deadlines) are high.

RELATED TITLES: Shift leader, lead supervisor.
ADVANCEMENT: This position can lead to computer operations analyst or, with advanced degrees or credits, to other management positions.
EDUCATION: A high school graduate should have an associate degree and operations training.
EXPERIENCE: Two to three years as a computer operator will suffice.
PERSONALITY: This person must have leadership qualities in addition to being alert, thorough, and able to direct and delegate duties.
ENVIRONMENT: Time is split between the computer operation room(s) and the office.

TRAVEL: Minimal.
SALARY: $20,000 to $30,000, depending on the number of operators under the shift supervisor, experience, and firm location.
INSIDE INFORMATION: The competition here is high; many people strive for supervisory positions. Most of the work is with other people in the company—both higher-ups and subordinates. A good leader who keeps technologically current will thrive here and be a candidate for other operations or management positions.

PERFORMANCE ANALYST

This person regularly monitors and analyzes the performance of the computers, making necessary corrections or changes either to improve performance or to fix problems as they arise. Some time is spent at the computer console or with modifying programs.

For someone who likes the thrill of troubleshooting in a large hardware or software firm, this is an interesting opportunity. The ideal person will also enjoy working closely with others when making the various performance analyses.
RELATED TITLES: None.
ADVANCEMENT: Without additional training, progress is limited to the operations area. More training is required for advancement into other data-processing sectors.
EDUCATION: The minimum required is a bachelor's degree in computer science; desired is advanced training in operations research.
EXPERIENCE: Two to three years in programming, analysis, and/or operations is desired.
PERSONALITY: This person should be alert, have good powers of observation, and like problem solving.
ENVIRONMENT: The time is split between the computer room and the office.
TRAVEL: Minimal.
SALARY: From $20,000 to $30,000, depending on experience, company size, and location.
INSIDE INFORMATION: Because performance analysis is usually time consuming, occasional long hours and take-home work are part of the job. As with service positions, time is important here, which gives this job the mental strain connected to trying to meet deadlines. It's a steady, noncompetitive position for someone who is not too interested in corporate advancement.

CAPACITY PLANNING ANALYST

This person reviews and analyzes computer equipment performance and utilization. (Utilization refers to the percentage of time a computer is used effectively in relation to the total possible time available.)

Based on his analysis, he makes plans for changing equipment, altering machine loading, or other procedures. He may be responsible for supervising a small group of analysts.
RELATED TITLES: None.
ADVANCEMENT: From here, one can advance to operations management positions.
EDUCATION: Necessary is a bachelor's degree in computer science; highly valued are advanced credits in one or more areas of computer operations.
EXPERIENCE: One should have two to three years experience as an analyst or programmer.
PERSONALITY: A logical person will function well in this position.
ENVIRONMENT: A professional office is the setting.
TRAVEL: About 10 percent of the time.
SALARY: $20,000 to $30,000, depending on experience, company size, and location.
INSIDE INFORMATION: A good capacity planning analyst uses creative approaches in problem solving and enjoys the personal satisfaction derived from improving a system and its operation.

There doesn't seem to be much competition for this type of position, found mainly in large hardware and software firms. The reasons are probably the long hours, the fact that there is take-home work, and the deadline pressures that accompany this position.

OPERATIONS ANALYST

The operations analyst is concerned with optimizing the productivity of computer and auxiliary operators, as well as making full use of the machine's output capabilities. This person sets up new jobs, recommends the purchase of new equipment, produces charts and diagrams, and usually is responsible for a group(s) of other analysts or programmers. His work produces tangible results in either cost-cutting measures or improved efficiency or operation, and for that reason is noticed by upper management.
RELATED TITLES: Senior, lead, or assistant operations specialist.
ADVANCEMENT: This spot can lead to management positions within various computer areas and eventually to corporate management.
EDUCATION: A bachelor's degree in computer science is required; advanced credits in operations research and/or an MBA are very helpful.
EXPERIENCE: Two to three or more years as a computer operator or supervisor will qualify one for this position.
PERSONALITY: This person should be logical, methodical, and well organized.
ENVIRONMENT: The time is split between the computer operations

area and the office; this person deals with operations management as an adviser.

TRAVEL: About a tenth of the time.

SALARY: $20,000 to $30,000, depending on personal experience and training, company size, and location.

INSIDE INFORMATION: Extensive work with people in the company, longer than average hours, and deadline pressures characterize this position. It also offers considerable variety and interest: it pays well, demands creativity in solving problems, and provides the personal satisfaction stemming from involvement in important decisions.

OPERATIONS RESEARCH ANALYST

Since computers move faster than the people who operate them, efficiency in the operations area is of paramount importance. The operations research analyst uses simulation methods and statistics to evaluate and modify complex areas, (such as the assembly steps involved in the production of an automobile), where work flow and time/motion situations exist. He develops models and procedures; spends some time running the simulation/modeling programs; and oversees other analysts and programmers.

Essentially, this position is similar to that of operations analyst; the main difference is the use of a more theoretical approach employing more research-oriented procedures and approaches, which give the individual in it the leeway to be creative.

RELATED TITLES: Senior or junior operations research analyst.

ADVANCEMENT: This person can advance to operations management and, with proper experience, to other management positions.

EDUCATION: The minimum required is a bachelor's degree in computer science with credits in operations research; desired is a master's in O.R.

EXPERIENCE: Four to five years split between business programming and systems analysis is acceptable.

PERSONALITY: This person must be alert, intelligent, and good with statistics and math.

ENVIRONMENT: The office is the major setting, with some time in the computer room.

TRAVEL: About 10 percent of the time.

SALARY: $20,000 to $40,000, depending on personal background and company size and location.

INSIDE INFORMATION: This is a relatively noncompetitive area, and a number of job opportunities exist. Some after-hours work and take-home assignments are necessary since deadlines must be met. A good spot at the heart of the computer operations department.

SYSTEMS SUPPORT ANALYST

The systems support analyst is responsible for correcting operating system problems (errors occurring within the computer), generating new systems, and installing revisions. Hence, he must know and understand operating systems (instructions that make the computer operate), compilers (which convert "English language" into "computer language"), and related software.

This is a very technical position and carries with it mental pressure due to the complex nature of the work, which requires focused, concentrated work, usually under the pressure of a deadline.

RELATED TITLES: Support analyst, systems programmer.
ADVANCEMENT: Progress is limited due to this person's high degree of specialization. With proper training and experience, one can advance to project management or operations management.
EDUCATION: Required is a B.S. in computer science with additional training in operations system software, the internals or "inner workings" of the machines, and compilers.
EXPERIENCE: One should have three to five years as an application programmer/analyst and a systems programmer.
PERSONALITY: This person should be very logical and have an excellent memory.
ENVIRONMENT: The office is the primary setting where the systems support analyst uses a computer terminal for his work.
TRAVEL: Minimal.
SALARY: $25,000 to $35,000, depending on degree of specialization and company size/location.
INSIDE INFORMATION: Finding solutions to internal machine problems may not be that easy, and as a result there is overtime or at-home work in this area. The position requires close working relationships with other people in the firm, as much input is needed from various people when making corrections or developing new systems. Competition is not that great, as this job is found in both software and hardware companies, usually large in size.

SECURITY ADMINISTRATOR

The security administrator supervises and manages security personnel (guards and clerks) and is responsible for overall security, an increasingly important area. About one-fifth of his time is spent becoming familiar with the different kinds of equipment and techniques being used.

Computer theft is one of the fastest-growing problem areas management faces. As society becomes information oriented, the value of a firm's information becomes one of its greatest assets. Protecting it is critical.

A person in this position who can maintain tight security will definitely be noticed by upper management and rewarded accordingly. He will also enjoy managing people and working with sophisticated protection devices.

RELATED TITLES: Security analyst, director of security.
ADVANCEMENT: Security is a specialized area, one which requires constant supervision—there is no time for breaks or slowdowns. Additional training is needed for further advancement.
EDUCATION: A BS with credits in computer science or operations research plus advanced training in security techniques is required.
EXPERIENCE: Five to six years as a computer supervisor, operator, and analyst is acceptable.
PERSONALITY: This person should be sharp, responsible, thorough, and have good powers of observation.
ENVIRONMENT: The security administrator works with corporate security personnel, the police, and fire departments, usually in an office or the computer room.
TRAVEL: About one-fifth of the time.
SALARY: $25,000 to $35,000, depending on experience, expertise, and company size and location.
INSIDE INFORMATION: Found in large hardware and software firms, the position of security administrator involves substantial responsibilities, not in terms of daily work produced but in terms of the absence of theft or damage. For this reason, the pace is low-key except when problems occur. This person must be constantly thinking of new security measures, as criminals in this area are white collar, highly educated, and sophisticated. A real challenge!

OPERATIONS ADMINISTRATOR

The operations administrator reviews, changes, and updates procedures and methods within the operations department in order to ensure that this department runs smoothly and efficiently.

This is essentially a managerial job involving overseeing the operations of the department; there is some supervision of people within the area, as well as paperwork and report writing. The operations administrator works in a fast-paced, dynamic area, and must be able to keep up with the constantly changing environment.

RELATED TITLES: None.
ADVANCEMENT: This person can advance to operations management or beyond with proper experience and training.
EDUCATION: Minimum is a high school diploma with computer

courses or advanced training. Helpful is a BS in computer science or business.

EXPERIENCE: Two to three years as an operator, programmer, analyst, or in other related data-processing areas.

PERSONALITY: This person should be organized and methodical.

ENVIRONMENT: Time is split between the office and computer room.

TRAVEL: Minimal for seminars and courses.

SALARY: $25,000 to $35,000, depending on company size, location, and personal qualifications.

INSIDE INFORMATION: This is a highly visible post among upper management, whether it is in a hardware or software firm. Since it is a mid-range position in terms of salary, competition is keen. The person who is sharp, keeps his eyes open, and handles deadlines well will do well here.

MANAGER—COMPUTER OPERATIONS

This person oversees and manages all personnel and equipment within the operations department. He must be familiar with all the technical aspects of the computers and related equipment and must know his personnel.

This is the top position in the operations area, a highly visible career step that offers political status and power, in addition to good pay. Opportunities exist, but you'll be facing stiff competition on the road to most management positions.

RELATED TITLES: Director—computer operations.

ADVANCEMENT: This spot has high corporate visibility and can lead to other management positions.

EDUCATION: Required is a BS in computer science or related area and an MBA or equivalent experience.

EXPERIENCE: Several years as a computer operator and two to three years as a supervisor or operations analyst are acceptable.

PERSONALITY: This person must be able to deal effectively with people (up to several dozen people may be under his supervision) and able to handle considerable pressure due to tight production schedules.

ENVIRONMENT: The time is split between the office and the computer rooms.

TRAVEL: About one-tenth of the time.

SALARY: A broad range, $30,000 to $50,000, depending mainly on the size of the installation.

INSIDE INFORMATION: The good manager of computer operations must get along with subordinates as well as upper management in a constantly changing, fast-paced environment. He usually deals with unions (where they exist) as well as individual professionals. There is plenty of take-home work because of the need to think about daily assignments and long-term direction. Because personnel and equipment must be utilized to their full potential to meet new product deadlines, creative approaches must be used in problem solving. This position is found in both large and small hardware and software firms; thus many opportunities are available for the right people.

EDP AUDITOR

The electronic data-processing auditor participates in the development of new computer systems in order to specify proper audit requirements to be followed. He conducts audits of systems while in operation to uncover problems. Technical expertise is required; he also has some responsibility for other junior auditors or office personnel.

The main goal of the EDP auditor is to uncover wasteful practices that are costing the company money. These may be hard to detect, calling for someone who knows his way around machines and people. He will essentially work alone, enduring typical mental stresses while doing his work.

RELATED TITLES: Senior or junior EDP auditor.
ADVANCEMENT: With proper experience and business credits, one can advance into corporate management.
EDUCATION: One needs a BS in finance and/or accounting; desirable are computer science credits.
EXPERIENCE: Some experience is needed in general accounting, finance, bookkeeping, or data processing.
PERSONALITY: This person should be inquisitive and thorough.
ENVIRONMENT: The office is the prime setting.
TRAVEL: Minimal.
SALARY: $15,000 to $30,000, depending on experience, company size, and location.
INSIDE INFORMATION: This person is paid well and also enjoys the personal satisfaction derived from helping to streamline operations and save his company (usually a large software or hardware firm) time and money. There is not that much competition for this position, as few really qualified people are available. As computer fraud increases, this job will be more competitive, since it will become better known.

PROJECT MANAGER

The project manager's main function is to oversee computer systems projects by acting as a liaison between his company and the end-user. He is the person most concerned with smoothing over any problems that arise and making sure that the client, the end-user, is fully satisfied with whatever hardware or software system that has been implemented.

Obviously, this person must be able to work well with people in his own firm as well as with clients. He will enjoy being out in the marketplace and making contacts.

RELATED TITLES: None.

ADVANCEMENT: This post can lead to higher corporate management positions.

EDUCATION: The project manager should have a bachelor's degree in computer science or a related field such as finance or accounting.

EXPERIENCE: Several years as an auditor, financial analyst, etc., is acceptable.

PERSONALITY: This person should be aggressive and have good leadership qualities.

ENVIRONMENT: The work is performed in an office setting.

TRAVEL: About one-tenth of the time for user contact.

SALARY: The range, $20,000 to $40,000, is rather large, depending mainly on the company and size of work area.

INSIDE INFORMATION: As end-user satisfaction is what keeps firms in business, this position is vital and therefore readily visible to upper management. A good track record here—a list of satisfied, happy clients—can lead to future opportunities. Of course, a position like this is competitive; few job opportunities exist. But the right people—aggressive, quick thinking, and sharp—will find their way into these spots.

WORD-PROCESSING CAREER SUMMARIES

As discussed earlier, word-processing careers involve the entry and processing of documents (as opposed to names, numbers, and addresses in data processing). Most word-processing operations tend to be small in size, and the number of different positions is quite small too. There is no room for error in this area as the work involves letters, reports, books, and other important documents in which spelling, grammar, and accuracy are most important.

WORD-PROCESSING OPERATOR

The word-processing operator is required to know several key-entry tasks that are part of a regular routine. These tasks include knowing the various options available on the machine, such as centering copy, making margins even, capitalizing, underlining, and so forth. Keystroke quantity—the number of letters typed per minute or hour—is

important, as is being thoroughly familiar with the equipment or machines being used so as to fully utilize their capabilities.
RELATED TITLES: Senior or junior word-processing operator; CRT operator.
ADVANCEMENT: Progress is limited to supervisory positions within operator groups.
EDUCATION: Minimum requirement is a high school diploma with formal training in keyboard skills (typing, keypunching, etc.).
EXPERIENCE: It is desirable to have some typing or keypunching experience.
PERSONALITY: This person should be alert and have good finger dexterity.
ENVIRONMENT: The setting is a professional office.
TRAVEL: None.
SALARY: $10,000 to $20,000, depending on proficiency and workload.
INSIDE INFORMATION: There are many job opportunities in this area, since word processing is growing by leaps and bounds. The work is steady, usually interesting, and the hours regular. There are little or no hassles for those people who do their job well, although some physical pressures do exist because of typing throughout the day. All in all, a rapid growth area where experience can lead to supervisory spots and increased salaries.

COMPUTER TYPESETTING OPERATOR

Computerized typesetting is a sub-area of word processing; the computer typesetting operator sets books, publications, brochures, or advertising copy on advanced phototypesetting machines. Some of his time is spent understanding the technical aspects of the job at hand, since each job can differ in layout and composition.

This person will receive specifications from the client and adjust the machines to carry out those instructions. The key here is accuracy and good judgment on the first try, in order to avoid redoing parts of the job that come out too small or too large.
RELATED TITLES: None.
ADVANCEMENT: Progress is limited to supervisory positions in the same vein. There are few big corporations other than major newspapers and publications in this area.
EDUCATION: Required is a high school diploma with advanced credits in keyboard skills or courses in typesetting operations.
EXPERIENCE: One should have three years experience as a typist, keypunch operator, etc.
PERSONALITY: This person must be alert to subtle requirements in the copy to be typeset.

ENVIRONMENT: An office setting, with some loud "humming" of machinery, is where the work is performed.
TRAVEL: None.
SALARY: $10,000 to $20,000, depending mainly on experience. Location is generally not much of a factor.
INSIDE INFORMATION: There is a tremendous need in this area, as typesetting houses and printers need good steady workers who are sharp and accurate. They will be well paid for this regular and essentially hassle-free work.

9. SALES, MARKETING, AND RETAILING

Like any other product, a computer has to be marketed, advertised, and sold. But unlike most other products, the computer can't be sold by any good salesperson; computer sales require highly trained people who are technically proficient as well as sales-oriented. This need for technical proficiency also applies to the marketing firms, advertising agencies, and other outside vendors who help companies sell computers. Whether you're an account executive at an ad agency handling a computer client, or a market researcher checking into prospective outlets for a new software package, technical expertise combined with an understanding of selling is essential.

Since most personal computers, or microcomputers, are sold at the retail level, the first part of this chapter will concern itself with the sale of larger systems. The second portion of this section will focus on careers in retail selling outlets—your local computer store.

For the larger computers, sales are obtained primarily through sales contact, with inquiries and leads developed through advertising and seminars. The final sale, however, is still traditionally made by the sales staff.

SALES AND MARKETING CAREER SUMMARIES

CUSTOMER SUPPORT REPRESENTATIVE

This person spends most of the time in the field, selling computers or software systems and programs to interested companies. The work includes presentations at meetings and extensive preparation. Since a thorough knowledge of the computer—highly technical in nature—is necessary, the customer representative spends some time keeping up on all the technical aspects of the product(s).

There are excellent job opportunities in this area since the number of companies using computers is continually growing; large commissions are possible when companies buy expensive systems or multiples of lower priced computers or software.

RELATED TITLES: Junior or senior customer representative, salesperson.

ADVANCEMENT: With additional training, this position can lead to management spots.

EDUCATION: A bachelor's degree in marketing with computer science credits is required.
EXPERIENCE: This is an entry-level position.
PERSONALITY: The selling of computer products requires a special person, one who is as at home with explaining the capabilities of a computer as he is with discussing much simpler topics. The customer representative must be dynamic, outgoing, well groomed, and easy to get along with.
ENVIRONMENT: There is a high degree of personal contact, both in the office and on the road.
TRAVEL: Extensive, but usually limited to a certain geographical territory.
SALARY: It is extremely variable, depending on commission arrangements; an average base salary would be $25,000 to $35,000, with commissions making salaries of over $50,000 possible. And there are also other benefits which sometimes cannot be quantified—car, expense account, etc.
INSIDE INFORMATION: The pressure felt in this position—the need to produce in order to justify one's salary, compensation, expenses, and so forth—is typical of the sales area. That's why a go-getter is needed in this position, whether he is working for a large or small firm. Much satisfaction can be gained when the equipment is up and operational, the client having invested considerable amounts of money based on your presentation and recommendations.

SALES/MARKETING ENGINEER

The sales/marketing engineer is usually involved in developing new sales campaigns, researching market conditions, and planning marketing strategy. He works with sales statistics and economic forecasts and may be responsible for other junior sales personnel or clerical workers.

This is a good job for someone who likes working alone, analyzing data and market trends, and projecting new sales outlets and sources.
RELATED TITLES: Senior or junior sales marketing engineer.
ADVANCEMENT: This position can lead to management spots.
EDUCATION: A BS in marketing or sales engineering with credits in computer science is required.
EXPERIENCE: This is an entry-level job. Sometimes companies will retrain a good experienced sales person who has sold another kind of product.
PERSONALITY: One must be fairly aggressive and have a sense of creativity; the competition is getting keener every day.
ENVIRONMENT: The office is the primary setting.
TRAVEL: About 20 percent of the time, for meetings and seminars.

SALARY: $20,000 to $35,000, depending on the sales volume of the firm and personal expertise.

INSIDE INFORMATION: A well-prepared marketing analysis with recommendations can give the holder of this position much personal satisfaction; he may also gain visibility within the corporation. As the arena of computer marketing is fast-changing and dynamic, the ability to recognize and analyze future sales outlets accurately is a valuable asset to have. Creative approaches are called for as this job is a real challenge!

SALES/MARKETING MANAGER

The sales/marketing manager is responsible for overseeing the sales force, giving input, and making decisions on sales campaigns and major presentations. He may handle large or special accounts that require his experience and expertise. Some of his time is spent in keeping abreast of technical developments and new product lines.

As an effective manager of people, the sales/marketing manager is responsible for the bottom line: sales of computers or software. He is highly visible to corporate management, and as the bottom line increases, so does his remuneration, status within the company, and personal satisfaction.

RELATED TITLES: None.

ADVANCEMENT: This position can lead to higher corporate management spots.

EDUCATION: The minimum necessary is a bachelor's degree in marketing or sales engineering, with credits or experience in computer science.

EXPERIENCE: Several years as a sales representative or sales engineer is acceptable.

PERSONALITY: This person should be dynamic, outgoing, well groomed, and able to get along with all kinds of people. He also must be a good and inspiring leader.

ENVIRONMENT: Most of the work takes place in the office, with some road work when large clients need to be visited.

TRAVEL: 20 to 30 percent of the time, to make special sales calls.

SALARY: The range is broad, from $30,000 to $50,000. A good manager accumulates income in many different forms: car, expense account, perks, etc.

INSIDE INFORMATION: This is a potentially volatile job, with ups and downs paralleling sales and the economy. The tensions attached to the job are substantial; not only does the manager have to produce business, but he has to keep an eye on other sales-oriented people vying for his position. For someone with perseverance, nerve, a thick skin, and a sharp mind, this can be a potentially rewarding spot.

CUSTOMER SUPPORT REPRESENTATIVE

The customer support representative does not really sell computers, software, or peripherals. However, the sales staff relies on this person (hence the word "support" in the title) to fill in any gaps in systems they have sold requiring tailor-made programming or hardware. He is also thought of as a troubleshooter for the sales staff; he helps in overcoming the technical objections from prospective clients.

The support representative will talk to many people in the course of a day, looking for ways to help the sales staff close sales. Some will be simple solutions, but others will require much thought, research, and experimentation, all necessitating some at-home or late-hours work.

RELATED TITLES: Senior or junior customer support representative, technical representative.

ADVANCEMENT: This position can lead to sales spots with additional marketing training.

EDUCATION: A high school diploma with computer training is necessary; preferred is a BS in computer science.

EXPERIENCE: One to two years as a programmer is necessary. This position can be entry level with a preliminary six-to-twelve-month in-house training period.

PERSONALITY: This individual must be personable and technically competent.

ENVIRONMENT: Time is split between the office and client sites, working with the client company's people in solving problems.

TRAVEL: About a third of the time, for on-site work.

SALARY: $15,000 to $25,000, depending on experience and expertise.

INSIDE INFORMATION: The pace here is fast; time is of the essence since a client is often just about ready to buy, assuming the solution to one last problem can be worked out. For this reason, there is much personal satisfaction to be gained from being a part of a major sale which depends upon your ability to work out the last stumbling block. This position is competitive, since good sales positions can be the next step.

RETAIL CAREER SUMMARIES

The selling of computers to companies and individuals, both called "end-users," has taken a dramatic turn in the last few years. There are now thousands of independently owned "corner computer stores" selling mostly personal microcomputers in the $400 to $10,000 price range. As new manufacturers enter the market, more stores open up at the rate of nearly one a day. Even giant retail chains are getting into the act. When the dust settles, we'll find thousands of computer stores, each trying to capture a slightly different segment of the market.

The end result will be many new jobs, unheard of several years ago. But there are only a few job titles in this group, since selling computers in stores does not require a large staff of people with varied duties.

There are also computer-related jobs to be found in retail stores that do not sell computers, and information on these can be found in Part III. But here we will look at people working in retail operations selling computers, software, and accessories.

RETAIL STORE SALESPERSON

This person is responsible for selling computers to people coming into the computer store. He must know computers well and be able to explain them in "everyday" nontechnical language to prospective customers. He must know the product line, different accessories or peripherals available, software, and literature to complement the computer.

Since each sale may involve several visits by the customer, the salesperson must be patient; he is dealing mainly with people who are still somewhat skeptical about computers. He will have to go over material trivial to him but probably hard to understand by the customer.

RELATED TITLES: None.

ADVANCEMENT: A good retail store salesperson can become a store manager and perhaps someday open a shop of his own. He might also be able to write original programs for sale, as many small stores now do.

EDUCATION: While no particular degrees are usually required, the nature of the work suggests a high school graduate who has had sales courses and technical computer courses at either college or vocational schools.

EXPERIENCE: This is really a first job, but any prior knowledge of the equipment, software, and peripherals being sold would be most helpful.

PERSONALITY: This person must be outgoing, well groomed, poised, and very patient, especially with people who don't grasp computer concepts quickly.

ENVIRONMENT: The store setting can be small or large, cramped or roomy.

TRAVEL: Due to the small size of personal computers, a new trend is toward salary/commission salespeople who tote computers around to prospective clients. This allows for some local travel.

SALARY: Variable depending on the commission arrangement, but should start at about $15,000 to $20,000.

INSIDE INFORMATION: Retail jobs are competitive because the number of stores in which computers are sold is limited. Even though stores will grow and hire additional staff, there will never be large numbers of salespeople hired. The retail salesperson may be required to work some evenings and Saturdays, traditionally a busy day in the retail store.

RETAIL STORE MANAGER

The retail store manager is in charge of overseeing the operation of a retail store, including personnel, equipment sales, orders and payments, advertising, displays, and other retailing duties. He must understand the technical aspects of computers and be able to field any questions from customers that the sales staff can't answer. He also might have some light bookkeeping, financial, or other noncomputer-related tasks.

This is a position for someone who enjoys retailing and wants to make it a career. As stores grow due to the expansion of the market, managers may have the opportunity to benefit financially from increased sales or the creation of new store outlets.

RELATED TITLES: None.
ADVANCEMENT: A superior manager might be able to buy into the store's business, open a shop of his own, or take a position with a wholesaling company or business machine dealer in a similar capacity.
EDUCATION: A high school diploma supplemented by courses in retail selling, business, marketing, and computer technology contribute to the making of a successful retail store manager.
EXPERIENCE: He should have several years of experience selling in a store environment.
PERSONALITY: In addition to having a good business sense, this individual should be personable, pleasant, outgoing, and technically competent.
ENVIRONMENT: The store is the prime setting; some managers may have their own offices.
TRAVEL: Limited to the local area for promising prospects.
SALARY: If there are commission arrangements, the range is variable, but one can expect to make from $18,000 as a starting manager to over $25,000 as a seasoned pro.
INSIDE INFORMATION: There is much personal satisfaction to be gained from running a good, clean retail operation. There are also longer than average hours and fewer job opportunities, but that should not deter the right person.

EQUIPMENT DEALER

The equipment dealer is part of a nonretail computer selling operation. He can be a wholesaler, business machine dealer, or a person involved in another business selling computers or computer products "on the side." A person in this capacity buys, sells, and/or trades computer equipment—activities involving considerable financial investment and risk.

A most important consideration for the equipment dealer is knowledge of the equipment. Computer store salespeople know their computers, and in order to compete equipment dealers must be equally knowledgeable.

RELATED TITLES: None.

ADVANCEMENT: This is usually a personally owned business, so there is no advancing within a company.

EDUCATION: While there is no college degree requirement for this position, this person must have had courses in computer science, business, marketing, and sales.

EXPERIENCE: Several years experience in sales/marketing is a basic prerequisite before one considers opening his own business.

PERSONALITY: This individual should be outgoing and have a good business sense. He must know when to sell hard and when to sell soft, and how to get people to work for him efficiently.

ENVIRONMENT: The office is the primary setting, with warehousing sometimes a necessity depending on the volume of the businsss.

TRAVEL: Usually local.

SALARY: Variable, depending on demand, locations, business conditions, and size of firm. It's virtually impossible to place a salary figure on this career. But while a salary may be low, the combination of profits, commissions, and other benefits derived from owning one's business can make a dealer a very comfortable living.

INSIDE INFORMATION: There will be many long nights of learning, understanding, and perfecting the ability to sell computers when they aren't your main line of work. But as equipment and business machine dealers are quick to realize, computers are their future, and the time spent will be well worth it in the years to come.

PART III
AN INSIDE LOOK AT OTHER CAREERS USING COMPUTERS

10. END-USERS: A SPECIAL GROUP OFFERING SPECIAL CAREERS

Computer jobs that are found within the industry itself are only a part of the total picture. When computers are sold, whether they're giant mainframes or personal microcomputers, they leave the industry and become the property of end-users. This group is the ultimate consumer, whether it's the data-processing department of a large corporation or the homeowner using a small computer for education or entertainment.

This section will focus on jobs found outside the computer industry in end-user environments. While there is a wide variety of computer-related jobs available in end-user situations, the majority fall into five major categories: programmers, systems analysts, operators, technicians, and data-entry personnel.

These positions have already been described in detail in Part II; you should refer back to that section for information on salaries, etc. But since specific duties and salaries will differ somewhat from job to job, it might be useful for you to do additional research on positions in areas that interest you.

Organization and trade publications that are available in each of the work areas (publishing, engineering, medicine, etc.) will help you to see individual differences within specific end-user categories. For now, knowing in a general sense what these people do is what is important.

Whether a computer is being used for medical diagnosis or marketing a new product, in most cases people in all five of these categories will be necessary. Their jobs, and how they differ from field to field, is what this section is all about.

Let's look at what people in these five major positions do in general. We will then look at how these jobs differ in different work areas.

Systems analysts analyze a business entity, ascertaining its goals and problems. Then, a logical procedure is developed which, when complete, will enable the company to achieve its goals. Analysts are good at visualizing, understanding, and tying together the pieces of the whole picture, noting how present policies will affect future actions.

They create a logical chain of events which solve the problems at hand.

Programmers convert the instructions given to them by analysts into a code that is compatible with the computer system at hand. It's one thing to be able to analyze a situation and recommend a computer program to add up all the monies in inactive bank accounts; it is quite another to take that request and code it so that the computer will carry out the initial request. This is the programmer's job.

Operators actually run the machines, feeding in data, tapes, and diskettes, and getting out reports, labels, and other information required by management. These people know how to run their computers and accessories to produce meaningful information necessary to management.

Technicians are needed to make sure that computers (and accessories) operate at optimum levels of efficiency and to correct malfunctions when they occur, keeping down time to a minimum.

Data-entry personnel take the raw information and enter it into the computing system, either indirectly onto punched cards or directly onto a CRT terminal. Accuracy and speed are two important factors for data-entry people.

Programmers and analysts are applications oriented—that is, they are concerned with creating programs and systems to meet specific applications requirements. An analyst or programmer in education, for example, is concerned with creating programs that will accomplish goals very different from those in the publishing setting. Therefore, as a group, applications-oriented workers can find jobs on a wide variety of computers within their own area of specialty but would have a hard time finding jobs in other work areas. They are specialists in the type of applications they design, not in the machines they program for.

By contrast, operators, technicians, and data-entry personnel are hardware oriented; they operate the machines and feed in the data and really aren't concerned with the nature of the data. An operator or technician can work in a financial, governmental, or medical setting without having to learn much new material. However, workers in this area are limited by the machine they operate; they can work in any work sector providing the machine they know is available.

These two groups have career choices based on either the applications they specialize in or the machine they work with. But since operators, technicians, and data-entry people do basically the same things in all work sectors, I won't analyze them separately here. To find out more about these positions you should read about them in Part II.

In this section we will take a look at applications-oriented people—analysts and programmers—and see what they do differently in each of twelve work areas.

It might make a lot of sense to think of computer careers outside the computer industry as two careers in one: your job (programmer, analyst, etc.) and the work area (finance, marketing, education, etc.) you choose to pursue. With training in your favorite work area plus a computer education, you can be part of two worlds at once.

11. CAREERS IN TWELVE DIFFERENT WORK AREAS

WORK AREA #1: MANUFACTURING

This is probably the largest work area, encompassing every product that is produced, from steel to soap. Anything that is manufactured requires most or all of these operations:

* acquiring raw materials
* combining raw materials with each other, labor, and other processes to create a finished product
* packaging, marketing, and selling the product
* inventorying, packing, shipping, and delivery of the product
* collecting monies, paying bills, meeting employee payrolls, and showing profit.

The job of computer people in manufacturing is to solve problems in each of these areas. One programmer might create a program to estimate productions costs; another might work on an inventory management system, using math and statistics; and another might design a process control system—programs that control assembly lines, robots, and in general make the production of the finished product run smoothly and efficiently. Your work in computing in the manufacturing arena can be extremely varied, depending on your particular area of interest and the needs and size of the company you work for.

Analysts and programmers in manufacturing must be knowledgeable in such inventory techniques as FIFO, LIFO (First-In, First-Out; Last-In, First-Out), etc., plus the computer languages being used (usually COBOL and FORTRAN). A lot of on-line program design (creating programs that will work from remote geographical areas, such as plants or factories located in rural or non-populated areas) is important, and graphics techniques are rapidly becoming essential.

COMPUTING IN MANUFACTURING: AN INSIDE LOOK
Michael Sumwalt
At the Heart of Manufacturing

Few people realize what goes into an assembly line, whether it produces cars, lamps, or bottles of soda. It's really a complicated process, and without computers today's volume of production would be impossible. Michael is a programmer who has worked with many manufacturing firms. Formerly with a company producing pumps, he is now with a major producer of computers, and is responsible for developing and implementing programs that handle the two key areas of manufacturing: production and inventory.

Mike is concerned with being able to figure out instantly what inventory levels are for raw materials, finished goods, parts on order, and so forth. Knowing highs and lows can assure a smooth, continuous production schedule and also help guarantee his company doesn't run into bottlenecks and delays because supplies of parts run out.

The other major area of his job is monitoring work in progress by predicting how many units will be produced by a given date or reporting on their current status, thus making sure all costs are in line.

According to Michael, good solid training in manufacturing is first in importance for his job; a computer background is secondary. He says, "In the manufacturing area, you have to understand manufacturing as well as you do programming." This points up the need, in many cases, for a dual education—a background in computers and the work area of your choice.

WORK AREA #2: PUBLISHING/COMMUNICATIONS

Computers have long been used in some areas of publishing and printed communications, but in other areas their use is relatively new. In both, they are fascinating!

Computers in this work area are used to maintain mailing lists of all kinds, including prospective book buyers and magazine subscribers. Statistics, demographic analysis, and sampling techniques are used via computer in order to reach specific portions of the population. Ever wonder about the bingo cards found in many magazines—the ones where you circle numbers to get information? That's another use of the computer in modern-day communications.

Other newer uses for the computer in this area include word processing for the preparation of copy for magazines and books, and typesetting. The trend is toward having the author or writer create his story or book on the computer, transmit it to the publisher, who in turn edits it (still on the TV screen) and then transmits the final copy direct to the typesetter over the telephone lines. This process avoids costly and time-consuming retyping.

Perhaps the hottest aspect of this work area is electronic communications, involving the transmission of information and correspondence of all kinds—from one-page letters to lengthy reports—from one computer to another, across thousands of miles, in seconds. The documents are stored in a computer at each end, and printed copies are available. The use of electronic communications is changing every work area I will be discussing.

People entering this area have an additional choice beyond being in publishing/communications: that of being user or job oriented. Job-oriented people don't really have to care about the data they work with. They put a mailing list into the computer and produce labels. User-oriented people, however, must pay careful attention to the data they work with. Typesetters and word-processing operators control the level of quality of the finished documents they produce.

In general, applications people must utilize COBOL and assembly language programs, as this is a heavy workload (constant flow of data) area.

COMPUTING IN PUBLISHING/COMMUNICATIONS: AN INSIDE LOOK

Kit Cone
New Technology for a Small-town Newspaper

As editor and publisher of a weekly community newspaper, Kit is one of the first small publishers in the country to use the new computer technology in a big way.

Writers and editors on "old-fashioned" papers type their stories on copy paper, correct them and deliver them to the printer, who in turn rekeyboards (types) the copy into the typesetting machine and then, finally, produces type for the story.

Kit's hookup, a computer terminal at his office connected via a modem (telephone line hookup) to the printer, eliminates almost all of the above steps. A story is first written not on paper but on the TV screen, where it is edited, changed, and rewritten as often as one desires. The story is then transmitted (no deliveries necessary) over the modem directly into the typesetting machine (located at the printer), which produces the type. This process saves time, money, delivery costs, paper, and improves quality.

Many of the larger dailies already use this technology, but at the local newspaper level, few are in use at this time. Kit is planning to expand the use of the computer, a small personal unit, to set type for the advertising department as well.

Kit says, "Cost savings are enough to equal an employee's salary. In addition, there is a real benefit in the quality of our articles . . . the computer process enables our writers to insert a paragraph here or there, change sentences or move blocks of copy . . . all without the annoyance of erasing and retyping . . . or the old scissors-and-gluepot routine. It's easier to make changes, and the results are usually articles with more effort given to writing and less to typing."

Richard Baker
Information for Everyone

Richard is the editorial director for a company involved in one of the newest concepts in electronic publishing and communications: Videotex, the transmission of information and communication over the telephone lines.

Currently, a few information services now offer anyone with a personal computer the ability to access (gain entrance to) huge banks of information: everything from stock market reports to news; from travel timetables to catalogue shopping; and, of course, much more.

After becoming a member of an information service, you dial it over your modem and key in your password. When you are cleared, you have only to type simple instructions and information about hundreds of subjects will be made available to you. You can also chat with other members, leave messages, place classified ads, and much more. What Richard does is to oversee the consistent editorial content for his company, making sure subscribers and users of his network get the type of information they need to make them more productive.

Richard says, "This area [electronic publishing] presents some interesting challenges . . . there are some very exciting differences between electronic publishing and traditional printed publishing. The writing is more concise and allows almost immediate interaction with our viewers." He also notes that people who want to enter this area of computing should know basic programming, know how to express themselves in writing, and have a basic feel for the technical side of Videotex.

WORK AREA #3: MEDICINE

Computers are being used in three basic areas in medicine: patient monitoring, patient diagnosing, and medical billing/office processing.

The area of patient monitoring includes direct hookups between critical sign monitors, sensing systems, and computers to keep track of patients who are in various stages of illness. You've seen the TV shows and movies where the patient is hooked up to a machine measuring heart beat; patient monitoring is based on the same idea, but, of course, is not as dramatic and covers a much wider range of instrumentation.

The second area, patient diagnosis, is one that can enable doctors all over the globe to have the benefit of diagnoses of hundreds of thousands of patients. Workers in this area compile logical tables and historical statistical compilations in order to predict, within certain strict limits, what illness is characterized by certain symptoms. For example, a doctor with a computer terminal in a remote town can dial up a main computer when confronted by an illness unknown to him. After all the vital information is entered, the computer compares it against a voluminous file of cases and selects those which match most accurately. Computer workers in this area must know statistics, logic, and other related techniques.

The final medical usage area is medical billing and office processing, which includes the standard functions of payroll, billing, receivable collection, and correspondence handling.

Programmers and analysts in this work area face real challenges, as there is heavy on-line (direct linkup) work required here. Most of the applications are time critical in that split-second decisions are required. This necessitates the highest quality programming and design techniques.

Systems in this area are custom designed for the medical profession; applications people here are very specialized. You should be very good at complex situations and handling pressure, as these two elements play into an applications position in the medical area.

COMPUTING IN MEDICINE: AN INSIDE LOOK

Brian Huber
Analyzing Ourselves with Computers

Brian manages the biosystems division of a software firm that produces programs and systems primarily used by psychologists and people involved with behavioral medicine. His work, which is on the leading edge of technology, involves a system that can monitor eight different modalities (variables or parameters) including muscle activity, temperature, heart rate, EEG, and pulse, to name several. This information is gathered and analyzed by clinicians who can compare results among dozens, hundreds, or even thousands of patients.

In this area, generally known as biofeedback, Brian works with information that is personal: the data can be used to help people with either diet changes or exercise adjustments. Most other kinds of computer-generated data are used for nonhuman purposes (billing, records, etc.).

Brian says he "likes the accuracy of the computer as well as the ability to make a change [in one of the modalities, for example] and then see the resultant effect." His programs are structured so that he can then "change hats and do some other function, such as word processing, with the same data." We know medicine today as white lab coats, doctor's offices, and hospitals. A fixture in this environment in the future will be the computer.

WORK AREA #4: TRANSPORTATION

Whether one is concerned with transportation on the ground, in the air, by rail, or by water, the computer has its place in the transportation industry.

For instance, one of the biggest problems facing transportation people is the need to bring together shipments and carriers in an efficient way. It doesn't do anyone much good to have empty trucks or railroad cars because shipments aren't available for them. The use of the computer in this area has made the connection between shippers and carriers much simpler and more efficient. Programmers and analysts design systems to match shipments with available modes of transportation.

But that's only one aspect of the computer's use in transportation. Traffic control, involving the use of light signals and traffic patterns, uses linear programming techniques to help create the signal timing and changes. Every traffic light is controlled by computer-related technology developed by people employed in this area.

Another way in which the computer is used is in toll-collection processing; the computer not only keeps track of receipts but it analyzes traffic from various points of entry through telecommunications programming (getting information from the toll booths along a major parkway into a central computer for analysis). The computer is used in a related way for air traffic control (juggling aircraft in and around airports), railway systems (switching trains, tracks and schedules), and naval operations (scheduling ships through waterways and ports).

Finally, the computer is used for reservation systems of all kinds, from airline tickets to complicated shipping routes with ten or twenty stopovers.

Applications people in this area are required to be very good thinkers and to work well under pressure. The nature of programming and analysis here is complex due to the second-by-second nature of the systems involved. Time loss and errors usually carry serious consequences; therefore, machines and software are critical.

COMPUTING IN TRANSPORTATION: AN INSIDE LOOK

John Rybacki
Keeping People Moving with Computers

As you probably know, the heart of all the major airlines' reservations systems is the computer, enabling agents to access and give customers information instantly.

John Rybacki is a senior computer systems analyst with a major airline, working on developing programs that handle reservations and fare information. He works with systems that keep track of an airline's inventory: flight schedules, reservations, cargo shipments, seat selections, loading times, transfers, destinations, and so on. He also deals with related information systems, so that his agents can give out information on hotel reservations, car rentals, tours, and the like.

"Without computers," says John, "not only would I not have a job, but the working of the airline industry would be virtually impossible. We create systems and programs to make it possible for our staff to gain information to help customers immediately."

Between figuring fares and connecting flights and times, getting a passenger from L.A. to New York with a stopover in Chicago is quite complicated. With the computer, it becomes possible to deal with these details in a smooth, efficient, and accurate manner.

WORK AREA #5: GOVERNMENT

Government—whether at the local, state, or federal level—has to have the ability to collect monies and spend them. Without computers, this ability would be severely hampered, since the day-to-day work of government involves huge numbers of people, collections, and expenditures, all of which need to be tracked properly.

Computer people working in this area need a solid background in accounting, statistics, and data-base management. Whether one is dealing with the property tax records of a town with 534 residents or with the nationwide census, the work is essentially the same, varying only with the size of the data base (and hence the equipment needed) and the type of information (reports, statistical analyses, etc.).

There are four major areas of computer usage in government. The first area is taxation, which includes tax computation, collection, auditing, storage, and analysis. A heavy accounting and statistics knowledge is required in this area.

The second area is census processing—keeping track of all the people and business enterprises in our country. The government has at its disposal huge amounts of demographic information, which it makes available to business and educational institutions. This data is based on census tabulations and analysis, again work requiring a good background in statistics.

The third area of computer usage in government is general record keeping and finance, which includes budgets of all kinds, inventories for all branches of the government, and personnel information (payroll, pension, etc.).

Lastly is criminal violations data-base management, which involves the maintenance of huge amounts of data on criminals and their places of incarceration. In addition to heavy record keeping, there is a need here for on-line (direct linkup) programming and analysis, so that law-enforcement agencies around the country can communicate with each other in the tracking of people.

Most government applications systems are designed and written in COBOL, which is a standard government language. COBOL is best suited for government work because most of it involves heavy record processing or statistics. Typically, government work requires very extensive documentation (written instructions) in its systems, which puts additional reqirements on analysts and programmers.

COMPUTING IN GOVERNMENT: AN INSIDE LOOK

Marvin White
Keeping Track of People

The census is something we all think about once every ten years, but to many people it is an everyday job involving the heavy use of computers. Tabulating over 200 million people's records and demographic information is a task that requires not only huge mainframe computers capable of "number crunching" (working with huge amounts of data), but people knowledgeable in extensive mathematical and statistical theories and formulations.

Marvin, an applied mathematics researcher, is concerned with solving census problems; he develops theories, models, and computer systems to carry out projected solutions. One example he is currently working on is the computerization of maps, which requires a mathematical model to be built, from which maps can be produced.

"Nearly every job gets some help from computers," says Marvin, referring to all the controlling operations the Census Bureau's computers handle: keeping track of our population, noting trends, and providing businesses with data on population shifts.

His fascination with computers stems from "their intrinsic nature, in that the machines are so mathematically and logically constructed." His interest in computers, he says, "stems from my early interest in thinking through problems logically." As we will continue to see, computers help people in two ways: by completing huge amounts of work . . . and by exercising the mind!

WORK AREA #6: SERVICE

Our section on manufacturing concerned itself with companies that produced tangible products you could see or hold. The service sector is comprised of those businesscs providing a wide range of services, from package delivery to insurance, from preparing a payroll to setting up a printing job, and so on.

All of these businesses are characterized by the fact that they handle information as opposed to a product like a car or a can of tuna fish. People involved in service are concerned with processing information and getting it from one place to another; or with using printed information to serve others. As you already know, one of the computer's strong points is the handling and manipulation of information, and the service sector benefits immensely from this capability.

Service companies are of two kinds. One uses the computer to provide data (such as payrolls, mailing labels, etc.); the other uses the computer to makes its own particular service more efficient.

The first division of the service sector is more concrete in the training its workers require. This area is comprised of companies that, for a fee, use their own computers to produce payrolls, invoices, statements, accounting ledgers, mailing lists, financial data, and so forth.

These companies require individuals fluent in COBOL, BASIC and Assembly languages. Machines used are for general purposes; some companies use specialized machines such as scanners.

Since achieving a low error level is extremely important here, programs used are usually quite complex, even though they must be general in nature and flexible in design. This is somewhat of a contradiction, but finding a balance between flexibility and specific requirements is a challenge in this area.

Among companies in the latter group of computer services, we find the small package delivery services, which use computers to schedule pickups and deliveries, coordinated with airline schedules; insurance agents, who use computers to determine all kinds of useful information when preparing policies; and advertising agencies, which use computers to analyze the best publications in which to advertise.

It is impossible to determine exactly what type of training workers in this latter area require, because the businesses are so diverse in nature. However, a good general knowledge of design and programming of systems is required. Workers in service sectors must be flexible and alert enough to be able to design the type of system required, even though they may not be specifically trained in that area.

COMPUTING IN SERVICE: AN INSIDE LOOK

John Messina
Software for the Insurance Industry

John works in the computer services division of an insurance company, developing and marketing insurance programs for larger insurance firms and creating on-line systems (linked by phone lines) for smaller insurance firms.

His company provides a complete range of services for the clients it serves. Since the insurance business is virtually all numbers, the ability to have either your own computer system or a linkup with a larger system is a major advantage.

John is the project manager; he directs programmers and analysts, whether they are creating a custom software package or providing services to smaller companies. He is responsible for starting with "a phone call from a client" to "the final product—the specific information a client needs to help his business run efficiently." The large-scale, high-speed computer, he estimates, can do the work of thousands of people with great accuracy in a matter of days, or even hours, provided it is programmed correctly. This, of course, keeps policy costs and operating expenses down.

Gene Fornarotto
Keeping Financial Information Flowing

Gene is the president of a service firm that provides computer consulting and data-processing services to the financial sector, our next area to be profiled.

His company specializes in record-keeping services for banks, unions, pension funds, accounting firms, and lawyers. Here's another example of how the computer aids in handling huge numbers of transactions. Gene estimates the cost without a computer to perform the same services would be "a minimum of twenty times greater, which would lead to much lower profitability through increased costs for my clients."

I think you can guess what that really means—these costs would eventually be passed along, in some fashion, to the consumer.

WORK AREA #7: FINANCIAL

Wherever there's a substantial amount of number crunching—working with numbers in such environments as the stock exchange or banks—the computer is not far behind.

As a very simple illustration, my business is a one-person advertising agency. Once a month, before I purchased a computer, I did my financial accounting work by hand; it took five hours to put all the numbers in the right columns, add them all up, and so forth. The same task now takes only thirty minutes, and everything always comes out right—no addition errors ever!

The financial community uses computers for a wide variety of applications, but they all involve the processing of large numbers of figures, whether we're talking about the stock exchanges, with millions of transactions per exchange per day, the banks, with billions of checks and other documents per year, or insurance firms, with seemingly zillions of figures.

Without computers, the financial sector of our economy would be light-years behind all others. But, of course, that isn't the case.

Computers are used in four major areas of the financial sector. The first is financial instrument analysis and processing, which includes stocks, bonds, savings accounts, checking accounts, certificates, etc. Whether it be a brokerage house's daily transactions, a newspaper's daily advertising revenue, or a bank's daily deposits and withdrawals, all transactions must be recorded, processed, and analyzed. They also have to be "proven" (checked for errors) within a short period of time, usually no more than one to three days.

Record processing involves handling all these transactions, but that is only half of this first area. The other portion is the analysis of the financial transactions. By applying statistics, analyzing historical precedents and using forecasting techniques, the computer people in this environment have the tools to analyze, predict, and influence extremely complex financial dealings.

The second area within the financial sector involving the use of computers is financial modeling and forecasting. People working in this area are involved in taking a company's financial data and combining it with economic indicators to prepare short- and long-term financial models and predictions. This is done to forecast and chart the growth of a company and establish prudent guidelines and strategies for borrowing and repaying monies necessary to a firm's growth.

Another of the number crunching areas in the financial world is that of pension planning and account maintenance. Applications workers here are concerned with investing monies contributed by both the employer and employee in the best possible manner to achieve certain yields over the long term.

The final area, certainly not the least important, is basic accounting and paying fuctions: general ledger work, payrolls, disbursements, and so forth. Workers here need a background in accounting to best handle the applications requirements.

Most finance systems are COBOL oriented, since heavy record processing is usually involved. Forecasting and modeling often utilizes other languages, including FORTRAN, ALGOL, and BASIC. Programmers and analysts in the financial sector should really like working with numbers in order to be most happy.

A concept gaining much popularity, saving extraordinary amounts of time, and yielding instant information is the "what/if" analysis. Simply, assume you have a complex set of data about a business: interest rates, outstanding debt, inventories, production, stock, cash on hand, and so on. All of these factors are interrelated.

You can now ask the question, "What if interest rates change from 16 percent to 16.5 percent?" The computer will instantly recompute every single figure which depends on the interest rate.

Suppose you want to know what happens if the price of raw materials goes from $3 to $4 per pound. Again, just enter the new price, and all corresponding figures will be changed. After you consider this concept, you will see how incredibly powerful it is.

COMPUTING AND FINANCE: AN INSIDE LOOK

Beverley Sherrid
Making Financial Numbers Meaningful

Beverley works in the financial analysis department of a major book publisher evaluating the company's financial operations.

Most people don't realize there's a lot more to publishing than writing and printing attractive-looking books. Beverley takes the records of all the books owned by her company, both those already published and those awaiting publication. These records (sales figures, publishing history, costs, etc.) come from many places—"not only accounting records but also our people's desk drawers, backs of envelopes, huge manila folders. My job is to combine this raw information and produce meaningful information for management."

The information produced from this raw data includes sales forecasts, production cost estimates, inventory counts, profit and loss estimation, and performance analysis. Summing it up quite simply, Beverley says, "The computer makes order out of disorder. Keeping track of all of this information without a computer would be chaotic."

WORK AREA #8: CONSTRUCTION

Workers involved in the creation of systems and programs for this industry are concerned with designing buildings and other structures, creating blueprints and other plans, and estimating costs. Their goal is to build safe, well-made projects that meet cost and time estimates.

Applications people involved in job estimating have to combine the costs of raw materials and labor with financing and interest rates over a one- to three-year period to determine the total cost of a job. Complex tables and intricate formulas are used to obtain these projections.

The trend today is toward using computerized graphics systems for solving design problems. Designers and programmers look at graphic representations of their problems. The use of color enhances this further, enabling hue, value, shade, and shadow studies.

COMPUTING AND CONSTRUCTION: AN INSIDE LOOK

Elizabeth Heisler
Using Computers to Create Skyscrapers

Elizabeth is an architect who works for a major architectural design firm in the design of large-scale construction projects. Her use of the computer is primarily for design, but other people in her firm use it for zoning analysis, structural analysis, budget analysis and accounting, construction specifications, and cost estimation. Those people working on design and structural analysis of buildings are almost always architects or engineers.

Graphics are important in Elizabeth's work. She uses a device called a plotter, which, when linked to a computer, can create scale drawings. She works with dials on the screen, similar in operation to the childhood game "Etch a Sketch," where pictures are drawn on plastic using dials to move the pen in different directions.

Of course, unlike sketching, her work is complex, involving the study and diagramming of building plans, elevations, sections, and perspective sketches. Additionally, zoning restrictions and requirements must also be included.

According to Elizabeth, "the computer is a good tool for producing working drawings for large-scale projects. If we want to change just one item, we can see instantly how that will affect the entire structure." This sounds exactly like the "what/if" concept we saw in the section on financial analysis.

Graphics will eventually be used in all work areas, but architecture is one area where its use is quite out of the ordinary.

WORK AREA #9: EDUCATION

We talk about computers in business, in government, and in many other areas, but when it comes to education, the future of our country really rests on the imaginative and prudent use of computers in our schools. Whether used in elementary schools (where computing is already being taught as early as the first grade) or universities, the effects of the computer on educational processes are amazing.

There are two basic areas to get into here: computer-aided instruction (CAI), which is what all the excitement is about, and maintenance of school records, which isn't as exciting. The latter area involves basic programming and data-base management techniques in keeping track of student populations, test scores, teacher schedules, and the like. Proficient programmers and analysts with a general background could easily adapt to this record-keeping area.

Now, for the real excitement in computers in education. Primarily, the computer can be used in CAI, computer-aided instruction. As a supplement to a teacher—never to replace him or her—the computer can enable students to move at their own pace without holding up the entire class. A student can learn math, history, spelling, or any topic, including foreign languages, at his own speed, getting instant feedback to questions and answers.

The trend in the field is toward systems designed by programmers and designers using new languages that enable teachers and educators to write their own text. The systems must be so simple to use that no real computer knowledge is required. The work of applications people is in the original programs which can be adapted to specific courses by the teachers.

Computer programs used in CAI must be sensitive to any individual, regardless of his or her educational background. The computer simulates a good tutor, using extensively an "alternative tree" structuring. When a student progresses through the "tree," each answer he gives, when combined with previous answers, gives the computer the next branch to proceed to and therefore the next question to ask. Therefore, every student's trip through the tree is different, depending on the answers given and other relevant information.

In the advanced CAI labs and environments, computer people create the systems, and teachers fill in the text, questions, and general course material. The best people to handle the second stage are teachers, who have the experience and expertise and know-how to talk to students and understand what questions to ask. For people starting out, a teaching background plus computer credits would make strong credentials.

COMPUTING IN EDUCATION: AN INSIDE LOOK

Charlie Chubb
Teacher Turned CAI Specialist

Charlie is a former teacher who now works developing computer-aided instruction programs. He has seen the possibilities of CAI from the viewpoint of both student and teacher, having first taught seventh-grade English before learning CAI as a student and then becoming involved with teaching CAI.

He is convinced, as both teacher and student, that computers are where it's at in education. The two major benefits he sees are "no barriers such as embarrassment or feeling stupid, which bar the student from asking questions or replying to computer-generated questions" and the fact that "the feedback is instant . . . there's nothing to impede the flow of information back and forth between student and computer." Charlie also feels, however, that teachers are as important as ever in order to enable students to reap the most benefits from the unique combination of technology and old-fashioned instruction.

WORK AREA #10: MARKETING/RETAILING

Very few people realize what goes into the marketing of a new product, whether it is a word processor sold to legal firms, stationery sold to large corporations, or candy bars sold to consumers like you and me. Huge amounts of market research, data analysis, statistical work, and customer profiling all lead to the best possible route a marketer of any product can take to sell his product successfully.

Computer people entering this area should have a strong background in business and marketing, along with statistics and report writing. High-level languages are used, such as FORTRAN, PL1, and COBOL. Also used heavily are various statistical packages.

Workers here take data from questionnaires, surveys, test markets, panels, and other sources and compile this information. This is the basic first step. Next the information will be analyzed, which is the specialty of marketing. Here the computer is used in an attempt to profile the best possible customers for any given product, whether it is intended for the consumer or for industrial use.

When giant corporations decide to roll out a new product or service, involving millions in start-up costs, advertising, and promotion, it's only after careful research and projections have been made. The better the analysis, the better the final projection of sales, costs, and profits. Before the product even hits the streets, the break-even point, inventory requirements, and other necessary factors are all set. How close the actual results are indicates how well the company's plan is performing.

The other side of marketing where computers are used extensively is retailing. Here, while there is some use for forecasting, the major uses are to keep track of inventories, accounting functions, sales reports, and so on. The newest trend is to have the computer hooked directly to the cash register, so that the instant a sale is made, it is deducted from inventory and recorded in other places. Management can then tell which products are moving and which are not.

The selling of products and services becomes more fascinating when you utilize a computer to help chart a course; it becomes rewarding when actual sales and profits meet the projections.

COMPUTING IN MARKETING: AN INSIDE LOOK

Steve Krumenaker
Information Consultant

Steve's company specializes in analyzing market data and assisting companies in projecting markets for industrial products. He has programmers and analysts working for him who create systems that can extract useful information from large amounts of data.

According to Steve, "One of the principal advantages of using computers is the flexibility they provide. For example, sales territories can be designed so that the sales potential corresponds to the abilities and skills of the sales representatives. As personnel changes occur, "what/if" questions can be asked: "What should be the new quota if territory boundaries are modified?" "If a new salesperson is assigned?" To perform this type of analysis by hand would take forever. With the computer, Steve can ask an endless number of "what/if" questions.

The other major benefit is analyzing huge amounts of data. As the number of responses to a questionnaire increases, for example, the more useful the data. A sample of 10,000 is better than 500, for obvious reasons, and the computer has no more difficulty tabulating the larger quantity than the smaller. The only difference is perhaps a couple of seconds or minutes, depending on the machine in use.

Steve enjoys his use of the computer. He specializes in analyzing results, not in adding up responses or applying statistics to the data. "It makes our prime work—analysis—that much easier when you have a machine to do quickly and efficiently all the math and statistics."

COMPUTING IN RETAILING: AN INSIDE LOOK

Alan Weinstein
Retailer With the Personal Touch

Moving away from giant computers for a moment, let's take a look at a small retail store.

Alan runs a high-fashion better women's dress and sportswear shop in a fashionable suburb. He uses the computer for all the basics—inventory control, accounting, sales receipts, etc.—which frees up his time for other projects.

But what is most interesting is his use of his data base of customers. Each customer is identified by name, address, phone, salesgirl, and brands of clothing preferred. At various times of the year, he sends out personal letters to different portions of his list, each signed by the customer's salesgirl, each letter an original.

This highly personal approach, using an Apple personal computer hooked up to a typewriter, has produced plenty of business. Says Alan, "The key to selling, in our small store, is personal service. If someone can feel they're important by getting a personally typed letter, it gives us an advantage over stores that only send mass-printed flyers."

Bill Leh
The Power of Information

The flip side of the retailing coin is large department stores and chains. Bill Leh is part of a family-owned chain of three department stores in Pennsylvania. The family purchased an IBM computer in 1961 when computers were unknown to the general public, and added two other systems in the 1970s.

In the 1950s, the people at Leh's developed a merchandising system which classifies merchandise by type, category, and brand. Now there are over a thousand categories, and instant weekly feedback helps Leh keep a close watch on what merchandise is moving.

With the computer, which he terms "indispensable," Leh can spot trends, peaks, valleys, and other indicators specifically by type of item, such as bulky sweaters or arcade-type games. This information, which would normally take weeks to obtain, now is available every day, and helps in determining advertising and promotional decisions, markdown information, inventory control, reordering, and amount of stock required.

"When you consider we have forty-five thousand active accounts," says Leh, "you can appreciate the speed of the computer since it gives us a flow of information to keep our business running smoothly."

Leh also does what our previous shopkeeper did in terms of reaching selected customers. It's now very easy to aim an Elizabeth Arden promotion at those customers having a preference for Arden products. Whether it's toys or hardware, the concept is the same.

Leh views the computer as an amazing support tool and often wonders how department stores and chains can run without them. He says, "We can do so much more . . . develop new areas . . . aim our advertising and promotion at targeted audiences with the computer." Someday, we agree, all stores, large and small, will have computers.

WORK AREA #11: RESEARCH

When people think of research, white jackets and bubbling test tubes usually come to mind. Today's researcher, whether he or she is in science, education, or any other discipline, uses the computer as much as any other tool.

The research process, to be valid and useful, involves several steps, all of which make the use of the computer necessary:

1. *Organization of data.* In order for hypotheses to be tested properly or conclusions drawn, a large enough amount of data must be organized in such a way that it can be analyzed quickly. The ability to code data and search/select, depending on one's criteria, is most important.
2. *Analysis of data.* It's easy for one person to look at ten different people's answers in a study and tabulate and analyze the results by hand. But when the data base involves tens of thousands or even millions of records, the use of the computer is critical.
3. *Understanding differences.* Research experiments usually have a control group and a treatment group. Under rigid conditions, the results from both must be compared with strict guidelines on margins of error, degrees of significance, and other statistical ratios. The computing power of today's machines makes this task relatively easy.

If you keep these requirements in mind, you'll see how a computer is useful in research. Additionally, the computer is used to create models, which are frameworks against which real data can be tested or compared. The idea is to make up an "ideal" of what should be, and then test reality against it.

This relates directly to prediction, which is the final area in which researchers use the computer. With historical data and models, computers can predict most anything with reasonable certainty, assuming, of course, that the model and data were accurate and plausible.

People considering utilizing computers in research should have plenty of patience and be detail oriented. Their backgrounds should include a good understanding of the various statistical packages and high level computer languages, especially FORTRAN.

COMPUTING IN RESEARCH: AN INSIDE LOOK

Mimi Fahs
Statistics for Better Health Care

Mimi works for the National Center for Health Services Research, and her project at this time is the organization of a health system that will provide quality health care equitably and be cost effective. Basically, she researches the effects of various financial alternatives in the health-care field.

As to her own job, it would "be impossible without a computer. We are in the midst of a real revolution. People and society will benefit from the computer's ability to help us plan for better results, especially in the area of public finance."

Mimi also thinks, and I certainly agree, that the computer will revolutionize the work environment and the family, leading to more people working at home, less travel, moving, commuting, and relocating. As we continue to see, the computer's versatility, whether in the analysis of census data, health-care alternatives, or the family budget, will affect us all in a profound way in the years to come.

WORK AREA #12: ARTS/ENTERTAINMENT

Quite possibly the most fascinating area of computing outside the industry—and one few people know about—is the field of arts and entertainment. Computer-generated art, music, and graphics are becoming artistic rather than mechanical innovations. Who knows, the next "master" may be a computer programmer or home hobbyist!

Computers are of course used by movie studios for animations, cartoons, and special effects. (The recent Walt Disney movie *Tron* featured over fifteen minutes of complex pictures generated entirely by computers and an almost equal amount of backgrounds. Whether you like sci-fi movies or not, you should see this movie just for its computer-generated graphics effects.) Graphics are used in all the work areas we've discussed to create lifelike charts, graphs, and colorful representations of complex problems. But the arts and entertainment I will focus on here are mostly individual efforts: music, drama, painting, sculpture, plus all the forms of mass entertainment—TV, movies, cable, etc.

Big corporations don't dominate this arena. In fact, whether we're talking about developing and marketing a space game for the home computer or creating a new art form, the companies tend to be small; in many cases, in fact, they are one-person hobbyists, artists, and programmers producing new variations from the comfort of their homes.

If you're thinking of combining an artistic bent with computing, you should know this is a new field and, with the exception of commercial positions, probably low paying—unless you hit it big with a new computer game or other special effect.

Someone entering this area should have artistic flair, although it doesn't matter if you can't draw a straight line; the computer will do that. But you should have the imagination to be able to tell the computer what to draw or compose. You should also be versed in math, BASIC, and especially in the use of machine language (the most elementary language of the computer) as well as being trained in graphics.

Our interview for this section is with a young man who picked up much of his knowledge hacking around with his computer, reading, and experimenting. There is no hard and fast rule concerning schooling in this work area.

COMPUTING IN ARTS/ENTERTAINMENT: AN INSIDE LOOK

Tom Ball
He Writes the Games

Tom is one of the "new generation" of young people, totally unafraid of computers: by age seventeen he was able to program in several languages and created games that are currently hot sellers in the microcomputer marketplace.

He is the coauthor of a best-selling game called *Falcons* and is working on several new projects in addition to maintaining high averages in traditional subjects in his high school.

Sometimes it helps to talk to people who aren't yet out in the working world, because you get a different viewpoint. In the interview with Tom, we talked more about the future of computing than anything else.

He says, "There are so many computer fields that haven't been explored yet, and as new generations of younger people get into computing, more programs, both serious and entertaining, will emerge. These will have different slants, perhaps imaging the social trends taking place at the time."

Tom loves to be able to create and see his work, just as authors love seeing their work in print, or actors love seeing their performances on the screen. He says, "The computer makes it possible for people with artistic imagination who can't really paint or draw to create designs and works. It has a wealth of uses, and the arts are just one of many."

PART IV
EDUCATION AND PREPARATION

|12. EDUCATION

Now that you've seen the whole picture and read the descriptions in the different areas of computing, it's time to ask the question, "How should I prepare myself?"

Computer companies and end-user firms are quite specific about what they're looking for. Being ready for a computer career requires not only that you prepare thoroughly but that you know all your options so that you can find the ones that will be best suited to your own personality.

And of course you want to avoid the pitfalls. For instance, because of the current shortage of qualified employees, many students are able to find jobs before the completion of their study, before they are really well versed in their field. The jobs they find may be temporarily satisfactory, but they usually end abruptly when the employer finds out the new employee's limits. Adequate preparation is essential for real career growth.

To help you make the right choices for your career preparation, here are six important lessons to keep in mind.

Lesson #1: *Make up your mind to study computing thoroughly.* No shortcuts, please! Don't take two survey courses and expect to get a plum job in computing. You must enroll in a proper computer science program (or engineering curriculum with proper emphasis in computer topics) at an accredited college or vocational school.

The primary reason for a full schedule of computer-related courses is your future competition. While demand for qualified people will continue to increase, the fact is that the number of full-fledged computer graduates is also going to increase. Therefore, the employers will have more of a choice in the future, and people who are not fully prepared will not fare very well.

The second reason is that without a concentrated background you probably won't last in a computer setting; and if you do last, the truth is that you probably won't advance very far. Because the whole computer scene is education oriented, with an emphasis on continual learning during employment, only a solid background provides the basis for working in this environment. Getting "marketable" skills and expertise early on in your career will also eventually make a difference in terms of long-range salary levels. The better your background, the higher dollar value you will command.

Lesson #2: *Know your degree options, for while they may not seem important now, they will matter in the future in terms of continual rapid advancement.* A bachelor's degree from a computer science program or a related discipline is usually enough to get you into a company at the prevailing entry-level wage scale. However, acquiring a master's degree will qualify you for a very highly skilled job and make teaching in a college or school of technology a possibility. A doctorate will open the doors to senior research positions as well as top university status.

There's no need to make up your mind right now to go for a doctorate, but you should know that somewhere up the road it's a possibility that could enable you to pursue a variety of different directions.

Lesson #3: *Become proficient in English. An excellent command of the language is essential for communications and report writing.* Not every one of your courses should be computer related. The ability to write well and communicate with people is stressed very heavily by computer recruiters. In fact, it is of utmost importance. Why? Because solving a computing problem is usually a team effort, with input from people with various types of expertise. You must have the ability to work with people on two levels: (1) talking in "plain English" to learn what the problem is, how it might be solved, and what your role might be; and (2) talking in technical language to create the solution, test, and implement it. In order to achieve both of these communication patterns, you must write and speak well. The importance of good English cannot be emphasized enough.

Lesson #4: *Become proficient in computer-related math, including logic, numerical relationships and working with numbers and statistics.* Math and computing go hand in hand, and while you don't have to be able to add large numbers in your head, it is critical that you understand mathematical relationships. These are found in such courses as algebra, calculus, and sometimes geometry. The more math you have taken, in both high school and college, the better your overall understanding of computing and logic will be.

The kind of math you will study is "common sense math"; your interest will be in knowing how variables relate to each other and what will happen when one or more variable is changed.

Lesson #5: *Sample a wide variety of computer courses.* The math and English areas will give you the basics for pursuing a career in computing. However, they are just the beginning. In your first year of college or vocational school you will take a number of courses that will give you a peek into the many areas of computing. If you combine what you learn in these courses with your knowledge of the careers summarized in this book, what should emerge is a sense of what areas appeal to you.

But choosing a career direction cannot happen without the actual experience of taking courses, since you can't possibly know in advance what being a programmer or circuit designer is like. So before you declare your major, be sure to sample a wide array of courses.

Lesson #6: *Make an effort to get something out of every course you take*. While you may not find a particular course dynamic or interesting, you never know when you'll have to draw upon information learned in it. The nature of the computing industry requires that you be aware of everything that's going on, because sooner or later, two diverse topics or courses will probably be connected.

Even if the course is not immediately applicable or useful, make an extra effort to get what you can from it. It will probably come back to you in the future, when you'll wish you had paid better attention.

DECIDING ON A CAREER

The six lessons outlined above will help you to get the most from your computer education. And of course once you have decided that you're most interested in a certain area, you should meet with the department chairperson or adviser to examine what your full schedule of courses should be. But what if you're not sure what kind of career you want?

A useful tool to help you decide can be the computer itself. Computer systems are now available that guide you through the whole career choice process, delving into areas of satisfaction, values, goals, rewards, etc. After analyzing your answers and choices, they present you with careers that seem to fit your interests. Some people may be surprised to find hidden interests or to learn that what they thought was "their thing" really wasn't. Another benefit of using one of these programs is that you'll see a computer in action and get some hands-on experience as well.

SIGI is the acronym for a system developed at the Educational Testing Service in Princeton, NJ. Students interact with computer terminals in a one-to-one format. The student's dialogue with the computer results in an examination of the elements influencing career choice, the process of career choice, values, a systematic exploration of options, a formulation of tentative plans and testing them in very realistic situations. You will be led through a series of endless combinations of learning frames, participation sequences, evaluation procedures. If you take it seriously, it is quite a beneficial experience.

Many of these systems have, in addition to career description information, files on two- and four-year colleges, scholarships, financial-aid programs, national and local files, and more.

The addresses for SIGI and several other programs are as follows. By writing to them you can find schools and colleges where you might be able to use the program.

COMPUTER CAREER DECISION-MAKING PROGRAMS: ADDRESSES

SIGI: SYSTEM OF INTERACTIVE GUIDANCE AND INFORMATION,
c/o Educational Testing Service
Princeton, New Jersey 08540

GIS: GUIDANCE INFORMATION SYSTEM II
Alabama Occupational Information System
Montgomery, Alabama 35361

The GIS program was developed by the Time Share Corp., and may be available in other states. Check with your department of education, usually found in the state's capital.

WOIS: WISCONSIN OCCUPATIONAL INFORMATION SYSTEM
Center for Studies in Vocational and Technical Education
University of Wisconsin
Madison, Wisconsin 53706
Contact WOIS at the university directly.

MASSACHUSETTS OCCUPATIONAL INFORMATION SERVICE

This system serves high schools throughout the New England states. Many of the high schools involved in the program are open to the general public. Inquire in specific school districts.

Use of these programs, and others like them, has helped students clarify their educational plans and career goals. Because of the heavy involvement of computer companies in education, by press time there will probably be more and more of these programs in operation. Check with either high school guidance departments or college computer departments to see if you can locate a program convenient to you.

In any event, if you can utilize a computer career program, it will give you further insight into the fascinating world of computing.

DIFFERENT KINDS OF EDUCATION

Another choice you'll have to face is where to prepare for your education. The traditional college setting is one possibility, with private companies and proprietary schools offering alternatives.

The school setting you choose will affect how long you have to train, how much your training will cost, and how effective or valuable that training is when it comes time to start job hunting.

COLLEGE TRAINING AND EDUCATION

This is the traditional route for computer science prospects. Whether you attend a two-year community college or a four-year university, what you should look for is the same.

First, talk to the job placement people on campus. Find out how the graduates at that school are faring. Ask what is being sought by employers, and how the school meets those manpower requests. In short, find out how the school performs with respect to the employment being requested.

If the prospective school passes this first test of employability, talk next to the chairperson of the computer science department. Find out the courses being offered, the equipment the school rents or owns, the reputation of the school among employers, and the amount of time available for hands-on experience. As you can probably guess, hands-on time is critical. There should at least be enough equipment so you can work on a machine three to six days per week for at least one to two hours per day. Compare the type of equipment found against that of other schools you investigate. Obviously, a school with several different computers is better than a school with just one. You need variety in this area.

Next, compare the courses against the curriculum presented in this chapter. This model curriculum is a national program currently being made available to colleges by the Data Processing Management Association. See if your college offers at least 50 percent of the same or similar courses.

Talk to several local computer companies and see how your prospective school holds up. Be sure to seek more than one opinion. Also find out if a degree from your school has a better reputation than those of other schools you are considering.

There are now computerized services which match your personal goals and needs against thousands of colleges on file to find those best suited for you. Others search out sources of aid based on your qualifications.

For the college selection service, contact GIS (previously mentioned) or the College Selection Service (Box 123M, Princeton, NJ 08540). For information on financial aid, contact either Scholarship Search Organization (1775 Broadway, Suite 628D, New York, NY 10019) or the National Scholarship Research Service (Box 2516, San Rafael, CA 94901).

PRIVATE/VOCATIONAL/PROPRIETARY SCHOOLS

You've probably seen ads inviting you to "become a programmer in six months" or "study for a computer career at home." These ads are used by a group of privately owned schools called proprietary schools, which offer specific vocational training in many areas, including computer science.

Apply all the same rules to your proprietary school search as I outlined above for a college search, and add one more—perhaps the most important one: be wary of every aspect of these private schools!

Unlike universities, these schools are somewhat unregulated, and the chances for dubious enterprises greater. Remember that you are the customer, and let the buyer beware! These schools may be less expensive but may not offer as much as college.

In both categories of educational offerings, you will find some excellent schools and some rotten apples. I'm not suggesting which is better, though employers indicate a college degree preference in some cases. I am urging you to make sure when you write out your tuition check that you're getting what you need and expect.

A good idea is to make a chart listing the important factors already discussed under "College Training and Education" to rate each school after you have had discussions with many people at each institution. The avenue offering the most promise will emerge.

TEMPORARY ON-THE-JOB TRAINING

Many of the large corporations, insurance companies, and banks offer on-the-job training for high school graduates or for college students during summer vacations. Once you enter their probational program, they provide training in the hopes you'll work out as a long-term employee. Should you perform well, you will most likely be retained for permanent employment.

The main advantages of this route are that it is cost free (you are paid by the employer) and that you'll learn on the company's equipment and in their framework, so you can fit right in after you're hired. They're gambling that their training program will pay off in permanent employees who have developed a sense of loyalty because they've received a "free" education. Of course, you also save time. Rather than spending four years in college, you're working and training right away.

However, you are limited. You won't get the variety of working on many different kinds of equipment, nor the background of a college education. You may be well trained in one specific, limited area. Not having a college degree with broader experience might one day hurt you.

For example, at colleges you may receive training on several different machines or learn many different programming languages. You may work in designing, analyzing, and data entry. In a bank's on-the-job program, you might receive training in only one of these areas. It's a tradeoff, and you should ask yourself: Is starting to work without a

Education

formal education four years early worth the potential loss of income and advancement that comes with a broader education base several years down the road?

Here you must analyze your personal goals concerning a college education. If you feel it is not necessary, provided you can get good training and land a good job via another route, then don't choose college just because it's the thing to do. Now, more than ever, you must take into account your personal goals and desires in making your decision as to where to get your education. There is no right or wrong—there is no law requiring a BS or a vocational school diploma. The person you have to answer to is yourself. If you're happy, that's all that counts.

COLLEGE AND SCHOOL LISTINGS

Write to Peterson's Guides for a listing of their publications (Box 2123, Princeton, NJ 08540) or ask for them at your library.

The Annual Guide to Undergraduate Study offers detailed college listings and an easy index to help you find which colleges offer computer science degrees. You're given enrollment patterns, expenses, special programs, majors, and much other information. This guide can help you locate colleges that are in the area you want and offer the major you need.

Another guide Peterson's publishes is the *Annual Guide to Graduate Study*, available in several volumes. Book 5 includes information on engineering in computer-related specialties and computer science, and covers research facilities, programs of study, and much more.

Get acquainted with these two publications, as a lot of information can be obtained from them.

You might want to write to the ACM, the Association for Computing Machinery, for a copy of their *Administrative Directory of College and University Computer Science/Data Processing Programs and Computer Facilities*. It's a concise handbook that tells at a glance the programs offered and equipment available at each university. Write ACM at 1133 Avenue of the Americas, New York, NY 10036.

A booklet called *Educational Programs in Operations Research Management Science* lists colleges offering programs in this area. Write ORSA at 428 E. Preston St., Baltimore, MD 21202.

You can explore the possibility of study at home for credit through independent study correspondence instruction. Peterson's offers yet another guide in this area, with an important introduction on how this often misunderstood area works. Again, ask prospective employers their opinion of a degree earned by correspondence.

For a complete listing of private, proprietary, and vocational schools, write for a free copy of the *Handbook of Trade and Technical Careers*, available from the National Association of Trade and Technical Schools (2021 K Street, N.W., Washington, DC 20006). You're given names and addresses of these schools, institutes, and training centers.

Another avenue is to contact your state's consumer protection board, department of higher education, or similar agency for special booklets they put out. For example, the state of New York puts out a comparative guide to New York State's computer schools called *Check It Out*. At a glance you can get quick information in chart form on various colleges that interest you. Write to Computers, New York State Consumer Protection Board, 2 World Trade Center, Room 8225, New York, NY 10047.

To summarize, approach where you learn computing with a lot of care and effort. No one can say if a college is better than a trade school or an on-the-job training program. There are pros and cons for each area depending on your goals and needs. So start early, take your time, and be as thorough as possible.

THE COLLEGE CURRICULUM

With such an explosive employment situation, the computing industry is taking great pains to establish guidelines for educators and students. As technology changes and the needs of employers change as well, the education community must be able to keep pace by producing graduates with the right training and qualifications—not people who have last year's obsolete skills.

With this in mind, see how the college or school you are investigating compares with the recommended curriculum of computer courses provided below. Don't assume a course is the same if the title is similar: check out the content of the courses. Also, make sure your school offers good math and English courses, ideally with a slant toward computing in math and toward communications in English.

If your prospective school stacks up favorably against this list, you're in excellent shape. Of course, this list is not the final word, but it is an important set of guidelines from which students and educators can take their cues.

My purpose in presenting it here is to familiarize you with what has been recommended after several years of research, so that the courses you eventually take are relevant and not old hat.

This summarized curriculum outline is from a report by the Executive Committee on Curriculum Development of the Data Processing Management Association. It was produced in 1981 under the direction of Thomas H. Athey, its chairman.

SUGGESTED COURSE OUTLINES FOR COMPUTER SCIENCE STUDENTS

COURSE 1: INTRODUCTION TO COMPUTER-BASED SYSTEMS

A first course with a survey approach. Opportunity for hands-on experience. *Contents:* basic computer operations, processing concepts, input/output, memory/storage, data communications, distributed processing, computer problem-solving methodology, programming projects, future of computers in society.

COURSE 2: APPLICATIONS PROGRAM DEVELOPMENT

An introduction to computer programming, with design, language, coding, programming, and related areas covered. *Contents:* structured problem solving, programming concepts, the programming process, file processing, decision making, control break processing, table processing, file creation, and processing.

COURSE 3: APPLICATIONS PROGRAM DEVELOPMENT II

The second part of Course 2, but is recommended as a full semester offering. It covers advanced program design and in-depth learning of high level languages. *Contents:* design and graphics of systems of programs, program design, module design, advanced languages, the language at hand: COBOL, FORTRAN, etc.

COURSE 4: SYSTEMS ANALYSIS METHODS

An overview of the life cycle of the development of a system, from investigation and feasibility to implementation. *Contents:* system overview, documentation tools and techniques, logical and physical systems, information gathering and reporting, flowcharting, input, output, file media.

COURSE 5: STRUCTURED SYSTEMS ANALYSIS AND DESIGN

Strategies and techniques of structured analysis and design for producing logical systems. *Contents:* system development life cycle, documentation of the current physical system, model for new logical system, human-machine interfaces, design techniques and tools, testing and implementation.

COURSE 6: DATA-BASE PROGRAM DEVELOPMENT

This is an introduction of program development in a data-base environment. *Contents:* data versus reality, information space, storage devices, input/output, organizing files, direct files, applied data structures, data models, data language, terminology and concepts, networking, data-base administration, data analysis.

COURSE 7: APPLIED SOFTWARE DEVELOPMENT

Here one will develop the ability to apply technical, managerial, communications, and interpersonal skills to a system development project in a team environment. *Contents:* project management, task definition, analysis of current system, design of proposed/modified system, implementation, communications, documentation, user and operational manuals, formal presentations. A hands-on project with real life or fictitious case experience.

COURSE 8: SOFTWARE AND HARDWARE CONCEPTS

This is a nuts-and-bolts course covering hardware and software, developing a background in technical topics of computer systems. *Contents:* computer system components, main storage, input/output, bits, bytes, addressing, instruction sets, data representation, character codes, assembly process and language concepts, operating systems, data management, secondary and mass storage, multiprocessor systems, microprogramming.

COURSE 9: OFFICE AUTOMATION

Developing an understanding of support systems . . . their design, organization and administration leading to more cost-effective and productive information systems. *Contents:* organizational concepts, traditional and emerging office environments, data and records management, word processing, communications, data processing, interfacing, human and political factors, technological projections.

COURSE 10: MANAGEMENT INFORMATION

Here one develops an understanding of management information systems that serve the user-manager, with theoretical concepts applied to real world applications. *Contents:* general systems and information concepts theory, systems classifications, humans in the systems process, models for systems representation, data-base management systems, decision support systems, requirements for decision-making, applications of concepts with case studies, communications skills.

COURSE 11: ADVANCED DATA-BASE CONCEPTS

An in-depth understanding of data administration and systems development from design to selection in a data-base environment. *Contents:* data-base administration, staffing requirements, security, privacy, control, data analysis, design and implementation, data-base technology, hardware and software. Case study involvement with specific recommendations.

COURSE 12: DISTRIBUTED DATA PROCESSING

Developing an understanding of the difference between centralized, decentralized, and distributed data-processing systems and their relationships with the business enterprise. *Contents:* the three systems mentioned with advantages and disadvantages of each, applications, hardware and software, communications channels, networks, project planning, implementation and management, case studies.

COURSE 13: ELECTRONIC DATA PROCESSING (EDP) AUDIT AND CONTROL

To develop an understanding of controls in computer-based systems, and the various kinds of audits performed for information systems and operations. *Contents:* the EDP audit and its explanation and relationship with the computer system, types of controls, audit techniques, auditing advanced information systems, risk assessment, threat analysis, business results verification.

COURSE 14: SYSTEMS PLANNING

To learn about the planning process and the resources available to help create a plan to satisfy a firm's information requirements. *Contents*: business planning processes and cycles, management organizations, selection of systems projects, application software planning, staffing planning, hardware planning, equipment selection and financing, decision-making process, communications skills, formal and informal approval processes.

COURSE 15: INFORMATION RESOURCE MANAGEMENT

To gain a broad overview of the management process in general and information resource management in particular. *Contents*: fundamentals of management, organization, objectives, information systems management, distributed data processing, legal considerations, communications skills, personnel issues, career paths, stress management.

If you are thinking of entering business computing, these courses are also recommended: financial accounting principles, managerial accounting principles, quantitative methods, principles of management, principles of marketing, principles of finance, organized behavior, and production and operations management.

If you are interested in scientific computing, you should consider these courses: introduction to calculus, mathematical analysis, probability and statistics, linear algebra, discrete structures, and algorithms.

Examine your prospective school's curriculum against this proposed model by looking for similarities in each category. Also, you might show this model to the department chairperson and ask for a comparison.

As the supply of computer graduates starts to make a dent in the demand of employers, more attention will be given to matching job requirements with educational programs. As a student, you must look for a broad background that teaches you to solve problems logically and communicate well within the framework of computing. You are not attending school just to become a programmer, but to learn about the whole picture. That parallels the intent of *Getting into Computers* —the overall picture is so very important.

ADDITIONAL HINTS AND SUGGESTIONS

Your education and training for your career don't end when you receive your diploma and start work. Because of the nature of the field, continuing education is probably more important than your original training!

You'll graduate with the basic background to land a good job, which will offer career potential. From there, keeping up with technological change and new developments will make a difference in how you progress on the career ladder.

For the sake of comparison, think of the Olympic alpine skier who has the lead after his first run down the slope. He cannot afford to slacken or someone will take over the lead. Until the medal is around his neck, he must continually have the situation under control. If it's snowing or the slope is icy, changes must be made.

Similarly, as you proceed through the computer career path, you must absorb the changes around you. You're the skier, the industry is the slope, and your competition is other workers vying for the same position you are. Since we are in an information-oriented society, those who are on top of the latest changes will have a distinct advantage over those who don't continually educate themselves.

Fortunately, it is easy (but time consuming) to stay on top of industry changes. You should subscribe to several of the computing publications, both general and technical in nature. See the Publications Resource section, Chapter 15. You should also join appropriate organizations in your specialization and participate in their seminars, tutorials, conventions, and proceedings. The Organization Resource listing is found in Chapter 16.

Another source of education is seminars by vendors, so you can keep abreast of new developments on the system in place at your installation. As you become familiar with organizations and publications, you will find it's easy to seek continuing education. Do it!

You should also look into certification by the Institute for Certification of Computer Professionals. In all fields, central organizations administer tests to give credibility and respectability to employees in that field. It's another building block in your career. Write the ICCP at 35 E. Wacker Drive, Chicago, IL 60601.

EDUCATION SUMMARY

From selecting the type of schooling to finding the right school to keeping up with the industry after you graduate, you need to take an active role in planning your education. This chapter, along with the following one, is important for setting and meeting your goals. You might even want to go back and reread selected parts of this chapter so you firmly understand the decisions you have to make. Briefly, the following points summarize the educational process:

1. Your choice is from among colleges, private schools, and on-the-job training opportunities. Talk to employers about preferences.
2. Investigate each school thoroughly, questioning the proper people on curriculum, job placement, equipment, and experience.

Education

3. Use an interactive computer system, if it's available, to test out your personal goals, values, and characteristics.
4. While in school, become involved! Subscribe to publications, join organizations (many have student chapters), and become aware of the total picture.
5. Don't limit yourself to your particular area of interest. If you plan to become a programmer, don't ignore other areas of computing. You never know when knowledge of other areas will help you in your career climb.
6. Finally, continually educate yourself. Be the "eager beaver" whose thirst for additional knowledge is never quenched. Remember, those with the most information have the best chance of succeeding.

13. JOB HUNTING AND RECRUITING

Think of looking for a career as a two-way street: you want a career that matches your personal goals, values, desires, monetary requirements, location, etc. The employer wants someone to match his goals: an employee who's knowledgeable, communicates well, has certain specialties, etc.

Securing employment is nothing more than matching these sets of goals. The more they match, the happier an employment situation both you and your firm are likely to have.

Because the stakes are so high in computing, and because training new employees costs so much, today's employer or recruiter is very much attuned to getting only qualified people who will produce for the company.

You must keep in mind that having one or two of the above requirements won't qualify you for a job. Conversely, an employer who meets only one or two of your requirements shouldn't even be considered.

In this chapter I will provide you with the steps to plan and effect a successful job hunt.

STEP 1: DEFINE YOUR PRIORITIES

In order to get a well-defined sense of your own priorities and how they match those of potential employers, do the following exercises. Start by analyzing your own personal goals. Make a list, with first, second, and third choices for the following items. (Note: In all cases, the word "company" is used generically to include firms, educational and governmental institutions, and so forth. It is not restricted to actual businesses.

1. geographical location
2. size of company
3. type of company (hardware, software, etc.)
4. field of company (medicine, business, etc.)
5. product or service of company
6. average starting salary
7. future career desires
8. continuing education plans
9. travel
10. vacations
11. benefits

Job Hunting and Recruiting

Of course, you can't expect to land a plum job which meets every single requirement of yours to a tee. The goal here is to match up as many as possible.

For the above list, make your choices according to your feelings, not anyone's expectations. If you want a small company, put that down, but before you do, think through the consequences. A small firm may offer a wider variety of work experiences or a chance to grow quickly. On the other hand, you might be putting in longer hours, and smaller companies can fail more easily than large ones. It's important to think through the pros and cons in each case.

If working in a certain area of the country is of paramount importance to you, write that down. Try not to sacrifice, but also remember to be realistic. If you pick an area where you don't live now, you'll be leaving behind family and friends. That isn't as easy to do as you might think. Once again, don't make a quick decision.

After your list is complete (not just off the top of your head, but after you've thought about it), your next step is to make a listing of potential employers or types of employers who meet most of your requirements. You will want to consult Peterson's *Annual Guide to Careers and Employment for Engineers, Computer Scientists and Physical Scientists*, probably available at your local library. This book is of value, no matter which educational path you've chosen.

The first part of this handbook lists companies in your area of interest that require graduates at the bachelor's, master's, and doctoral levels. The companies are then listed by primary industry classifications (their products) and then by the locations around the country that offer starting jobs.

The next section consists of employer profiles, which give you the following information about each company:

1. general information
2. chances for employment
3. average annual starting salary
4. training
5. job-related graduate study
6. starting locations
7. international assignments
8. citizenship
9. summer employment
10. opportunities for experienced personnel
11. bachelor's- and master's-level opportunities: majors sought/assignments offered
12. doctoral-level opportunities: specialties sought
13. contact person

Also included are expanded two-page descriptions of firms that wish to go into extensive detail about their companies and employment needs.

An additional source of major computer employers is a booklet called *COMPJOB* ($6.95) from Employment Information Services, Box 3265, Chico, CA 95927. Also, your librarian might have additional sources of listings.

There is a lot to do before you start applying to companies, so make a good detailed list of firms that look good to you. After seeing what is generally available, and matching that against your list of personal goals, you can then refine your goals list to be as realistic as possible. You will find that some things you want are on target and others not. You will come across employment situations that offer many, few, or none of the goals you seek. The final objective of this first step is to get a well-defined listing of your priorities.

Now you know more specifically what you're looking for, and what companies in general need. A good start.

STEP 2: PREPARING FOR THE CAREER HUNT

Next, you need to look at what people expect from you. You should be aware of the following qualities that recruiters, employers, and employment agencies will look for in you. They are all almost equally important, so do not assume number 8, say, is not as critical as number 1.

1. ability to speak and write clearly
2. solid background in mathematics
3. solid foundation in computer science fundamentals
4. problem-solving ability
5. knowledge of the software development process
6. ability to work with people
7. managerial ability
8. poise, appearance, and attitude

In everything you do in looking for a job—your résumé, phone calls, interviews, follow-up, etc.—these qualities (or lack of them) are open to inspection.

For example, when you make phone calls, you reveal your ability to speak clearly and communicate with people. In your résumé, many of your other traits—e.g., organization (how easy your résumé is to understand)—are apparent.

Key to remember: you are always on stage, so keep in mind all eight qualities employers want. You might be surprised at how much employers notice. For example, one employer may place a lot of weight on how an applicant relates to her secretary. If an applicant acts superior or less than cordial, that may be a black mark right from the start.

Job Hunting and Recruiting

When writing to, talking with, or visiting a prospective employer, treat everyone well—you might accidentally bump into the president of the company!

When the backgrounds of applicants are similar, other attributes will make the difference in hiring. Intangibles will be important factors. Here's a brief list of extra items you will want to make sure you handle properly:

1. your dress (sharp and impressive rather than drab)
2. your answers to questions (well thought out, accurate answers rather than beating around the bush)
3. how you speak (crisply and clearly rather than muddily)
4. how you're organized (efficient rather than sloppy)
5. how you relate to others (sincere and kind rather than rude and arrogant)
6. what you think of yourself (top-notch person rather than ordinary person)

These factors often make or break a potential employee's chances. Employers are not interested in where you were born but in what you have done to help your previous company or what you can do for them. They'll ask questions aimed at your weaknesses. Turn them around to your advantage. For example, if you're told you lack qualifications, respond that you are a fast learner who is eager.

They'll be very impressed if you come in with a folder about their company, showing that you've done research. Imagine the reaction if you say something like, "Mr. Smith, according to Peterson's and the software trends, your firm would seem to need programmers with COBOL experience. Not only do I have that, but my school, Midwestern University, had a senior project with a COBOL on-line system. I am currently taking an IBM continuing education course on the same model you have here."

This type of talk shows the employer you're on the ball and know what you're talking about. It will win, hands down, over statements like, "Mr. Smith, I just graduated from Midwestern University with a computer science degree. Do you need any programmers now?"

If you have prepared a personal goals list and a list of employers, you're already better prepared than about 90 percent of the people looking for jobs. The effort is well worth it.

STEP 3: PREPARING THE RÉSUMÉ

To start any career hunt, you need a résumé. It's the written summary of your best selling points, neatly presented in an attractive package, usually one page in length. Your résumé is probably the first thing an employer, recruiter, employment agency representative, or job placement counselor will see of you, aside from an initial phone call. Giving a good enough impression to interest them in calling you for an interview is the first hurdle. Having it typeset (as opposed to typewritten) makes a better impression but isn't necessary.

When creating a résumé, think of yourself as a salesperson. You are selling yourself, the product. You need a personable, enthusiastic "sales pitch" about yourself, one that comes over as genuine. This sales message, to be done with taste and imagination, is useful in your résumé, and later when you go for interviews.

What are the basic elements of your sales message? Any good salesperson (and you should ask any people in sales you know) will tell you that the components of a sales presentation are:

1. knowledge of your product (you)
2. knowledge of your client (employer)
3. past accomplishments (training, degrees, experience, etc.)
4. current accomplishments (present job, outside activities)
5. how your product (you) will solve the employer's problems (how you helped solve a problem in school or on a present job)

Working these elements into a résumé and oral presentation is of utmost importance. Employers read many résumés and conduct dozens of interviews. Your object is to make yours stand out.

The résumé is usually a standard format, with information easy to read and pick out. There are many excellent books that show typical résumés for various positions. Buy one—it's a good investment. What you choose to include and emphasize is important. The following sections of the résumé should all be present, keeping in mind your goal to present useful, clear, and concise information.

1. Personal Identification: where you can easily be reached if someone is interested in you. Home phone, extension or phone at school, etc., and mailing and/or forwarding address. If they want to reach you in a hurry, make it easy.

2. Personal Career Objective: what your goals are, carefully thought out, and how you can merge them into the firm's needs. Indicate where you want to be in three, five, seven, ten years, showing knowledge of the company and personal ambition. Let them know you don't want to be an entry-level programmer for the rest of your life; but don't give the opinion that you're after the boss's job! Be realistic and enthusiastic.

3. Educational Background: be concise and brief, listing school(s), degree(s), major, grade point average, awards, honors, special courses or seminars, etc. Show that your training is comprehensive and complete.

4. Work Experience: highlight computer-related work experience

(summers, during school, etc.), or if none is available, show how other experience can be applied to a computing environment. If possible, tailor your work experience to the specific type of firm to which you are applying. For example, a business company won't be interested in experience you've had in nuclear reactor programming.

5. Personal Interests and Activities: show you're a well-rounded person by the trade and personal magazines you read, and your hobbies, sports, and interests. Employers generally do not want people who only know complex computer formulas and intricacies, but people who are knowledgeable in many areas, including those outside computing.

6. References: if possible, get references from previous employers (full or part time), computer department or school people, and people whom you have made a good impression on in the past. Don't ask a friend, relative or sibling—employers can see right through that. People you know with credentials, experience, or important positions can open doors for you by writing letters of introduction. See if you can have people you know do this for you.

Another document you will need to write is a cover letter. When you are asked to send a résumé to a prospective employer, a cover letter should accompany it. This letter should be tailor-made for the company it is going to. Show that you have researched the company by referring to its branch locations, type of equipment, products, services, etc. Even before your résumé is read, the recruiter will read your cover letter. If that doesn't make a decent impression, your résumé may never be read.

STEP 4: GETTING INTERVIEWS

Usually, getting interviews is the easiest hurdle to overcome, provided you are prepared and know where to look. Your approach should be multitargeted, aiming for many interviews so you can be exposed to many different kinds of operations, requirements, options, and environments. Don't jump at the first offer. Take a little extra time to see what many firms are offering. But don't waste your time interviewing with companies that are not up your alley.

You should explore the following methods of obtaining interviews, each of which can be equally effective.

1. Job Placement Office: If you choose your school or college well, it has a good placement office, which is actually a clearinghouse of employment information. Make an appointment with the person in charge, dropping off a résumé in advance and perhaps a short note confirming your appointment. This shows the placement officer you are professional. Indicate in your interview with this person what your

goals are and what type of company you'd like to work for. Show that you've done some research, suggesting types of companies you'd like to work for, fields of interest, and areas you want to stay away from.

Give this person ammunition. Give him information that he can relate to his contacts. The more positive information he knows about you, the more he can impress people he knows. Finally, give this person a listing of preferable interview times, and follow up your interview with a "thank you for all your present and future assistance" letter. This touch will go a long way.

2. Recruiting Schedule: Either available from your placement office or posted on bulletin boards (check with counselors or other students to see where these bulletin boards are located) is a schedule of company recruiters scheduled to appear at your school, with dates and names. There will be instructions on setting up appointments. If possible, see if you can drop a line to the recruiter with your résumé. If you can, do it; you will make probably the best first impression of all the students in your school.

3. Computer Publications and Local Newspapers: By now you've taken the time to become familiar with such publications as *Computerworld*, *Software News*, and other trade publications that carry classified employment advertising. You'll find the career advertising found in trade magazines and papers quite sophisticated, not like what you found when looking for a summer job as a kid.

Large amounts of money are spent on employment advertising, and these ads can be a good source. Write or, if possible, call the contact person mentioned in the ad. If you call, try to establish rapport with the person, and find out how he/she wants to handle your inquiry. If you write, check on the company first to make sure it meets your goal and value list. Write a tailor-made letter and enclose your résumé. Follow up with a phone call or short note two weeks later, making sure they received your information, and asking if there's any additional information they need.

Also look into your local daily newspaper, usually on Sunday, for more local employment opportunities. Follow the same procedure here.

Once again, the idea is to contact companies whose requirements mesh with your desires, and then approach them in a professional way, presenting yourself forcefully and appropriately.

4. Employment Agencies: When you look through the trade magazines and newspapers, you will undoubtedly see ads for employment firms, many of which specialize in computer employment. Some of the larger firms put out reports and surveys, which you should write for. You might even find some give a free analysis of your current situation and advice on where to look.

Job Hunting and Recruiting

The following listing of employment firms specializing in computers is by no means complete. *Computerworld*, the trade newspaper, has a large section of classified employment advertising. The list below is of companies that provide written literature and reports which are usually free:

Source EDP (2 Northfield Plaza, Northfield IL 60093)

First Interstate Services (411 N. Vermont Ave., Los Angeles, CA 90004)

Computer Resources Group Inc. (303 Sacramento St., San Francisco, CA 94111)

Placement Services, Ltd. (635 Madison Ave., New York, NY 10022)

Scientific Placements Inc. (Box 19949, Houston, TX 77024)

COMPU Search (607 Boylston St., Boston, MA 02116)

Robert Half (522 Fifth Ave., New York, NY 10036)

Electronic Systems Personnel (858 TCF Tower, 121 S. 8th St., Minneapolis, MN 55402)

RSVP Services (1 Cherry Hill Mall, Cherry Hill, NJ 08002)

Fox-Morris (7317 Mill Ridge Rd., Raleigh, NC 27625)

There are many other regional agencies in addition to the sources listed above, and some specialize in one area of the country. Consult the classified pages and your local phone book.

You should register with several agencies, making sure you know their policy on fees. If you have to pay them upon landing a job, take that into account. Many of these firms are paid by the employers, so make sure you know the policy beforehand. It's hard to decide which is better, but I'd lean toward agencies that are paid by the employers—they have, I think, a higher incentive to find and fill positions, and perhaps more latitude in searching for candidates.

You'll be asked to fill out an application and leave your résumé, or even several copies of it. In addition to these two documents, leave a short note summarizing the type of company you'd like to work for (a description based on the list you previously made up). On the application, take your time and only put down material that promotes and shows yourself off.

When the employment agency finds potential openings, they will call you in and discuss them. There's no need to jump into an interview with the company unless you (and the employment agency person) are sure the job is right for both you and the employer.

5. Job Fairs: Recently job fairs have become a very important way to make valuable contacts, especially for people currently employed who can't afford to jeopardize their current status. Attendees include people looking for employment and exhibitors (companies) in need of employees. The job fair has a convention atmosphere crossed with a

dating service—people seeking to match people with positions. Some organizations conducting these fairs prescreen applicants to assure only quality; others don't.

These fairs have been successful because job seekers pay nothing except for travel, lodging, and in some cases perhaps an application processing fee or résumé distribution service. They are usually held in easily accessible hotels and at convenient times and are well advertised in local newspapers, on radio, and through announcements sent to college placement offices.

At some of these fairs, recruiters present thumbnail sketches of the companies they represent, and from these presentations, you can see if they are right for you. If you're interested, a good one-on-one talk comes next, with a possible follow-up at a later date.

Job fairs offer a neutral site for the interview, which is also important. Bring along several copies of your résumé which you can leave with the representatives. One firm that conducts job fairs around the country is Business People Inc. Write them for their schedule at 100 N. 7th St., Minneapolis, MN 55403.

6. The Employment Register: The ACM Computer Science Conference matches computer scientists and data-processing personnel with employer opportunities for both new graduates and experienced people. The listings are nationwide, and this register is an excellent mechanism for establishing contact between applicant and employer. For more information, write ACM Computer Science Employment Register, Department of Computer Science, University of Pittsburgh, Pittsburgh, PA 15260.

STEP 5: THE INTERVIEW

Assuming you've done everything as recommended, you now have landed a slew of interviews at many companies. What next?

The screening interview, and then the final interview, are the critical tests for you. They are the last hurdles before probable employment. After a successful interview with a company representative who wants to make sure you would fit in, you will probably meet your future boss for one last interview. In any event, preparation for your interviews is most important.

The Peterson's guide referred to earlier presents two important lists that you should study thoroughly. The first includes the stages of the interview, what topics are covered during the interview, and what the interviewer looks for. The second lists fifty questions most commonly asked at interviews. It's probably a very good idea to work up practice answers to these questions so you're not surprised by them.

Keep in mind that the interview should be a two-way street in all areas. The number of questions asked should not be lopsided in the interviewer's favor. You should ask questions about the company to see if you'll be happy there. Find out what you'd be doing in your first job, what the advancement possibilities are, the equipment present, etc. The interviewer will be impressed, once again, if you show an interest in the company as opposed to just asking for a job or only focusing on what the company can do for you. And don't forget that the interviewer is human—he can react emotionally, positively or negatively, to qualities you show.

Once you've prepared your personal goals list, your ideal employer list, and have carefully read the references listed above, you should be able to interview well. At your fingertips should be well-thought-out and planned answers that reflect knowledge, research, and professionalism on your part.

Follow up the interview with a thank-you note that also asks whether any further information is necessary. If more than one person interviewed you, send the letter to both. (Be sure to take down names, properly spelled, while you're being interviewed. Nothing is more unprofessional than misspelled names.)

A few hints about recruiters. Recruiters are people whom the company sends around the country to seek out and find new employees. Their job, simply, is to find people who will make good employees for their company. They're proud of their company and are flattered when you've done your homework. The recruiter starts with a neutral attitude toward you and changes either positively or negatively, depending on how you come across. No matter where the interview takes place—on campus, at a job fair, or in a coffee shop—the recruiter is looking for a professional.

Recruiters usually can't hire but can highly recommend you. However, they can easily dismiss you, and once they have, for all intents and purposes you're finished with that company.

Generally, everyone will be treated fairly by recruiters. Your edge over other applicants is that you show exceptional interest, enthusiasm, and professionalism and have taken the time to investigate the company in question. Again, the preparation is well worth it.

You might be nervous the first few times, which is OK. Recruiters don't place much importance on nervousness, except when it is accompanied by arrogance and/or ignorance. You will find that you get better with each succeeding interview.

Finally, you usually should not take the first job that is offered you, unless it really is perfect. Set up many interviews with companies in different areas so you can have the widest choice.

It's a good feeling to interview well; you can usually tell if you've done well during the interview or immediately after. It's also a poor feeling to know when and if you bomb out. If you've followed my instructions in preparation outlined in these two chapters, there's only one more piece of advice I can give: loosen up, relax, and enjoy the interview. Don't be defensive, worried, or afraid! Remember, it's a one-on-one situation; the interviewer needs you as much as you need him.

14. WINDUP

How does one summarize all the information just presented to you? The idea for a final chapter tying together *Getting into Computers* eluded me until 2:00 A.M. one morning.

After processing (in my mind—not on my computer!) the various chapters while asleep, the answer seemed to come from nowhere, and eight words presented themselves. Oddly enough, the first letters of these eight key words spell "computer."

While these concepts are broad in nature, they suggest a nice framework for your career in computing. As your career is a never-ending process, these concepts will always be valuable to you.

Comprehend. Think, for a minute, about what will happen in the next ten or twenty years. To our society, to us as individuals, even to our world. Let it all sink in . . . high technology brings advancements at breakneck speed . . . a population behind the times in being educated about this technology . . . the careers open to you.

Observe. See what's going on around you. Be aware of what business, science, and people are doing. Be on top of things. Don't be the last to know. Be the first, and capitalize on it.

Maximize. Analyze your goals, values, likes, dislikes, and decide to gain the maximum potential in your career. This includes happiness, satisfaction, financial reward, recognition, etc. Don't just get a job; search out a meaningful and important career.

Probe. Go beneath the surface. Spend the extra time tracking down the right school. Make efforts to establish contacts wherever you go. Don't take everything at face value. Ask questions when you don't understand.

Understand. Know the hows, whys, whos, whats, and whens about computers. Get a good overall view, from a technical viewpoint and a social one. Know the effect of computers in almost any situation. Develop a computer sense, one which will guide you in your career planning.

Train. Get plenty of experience. Put in the extra hours. Sacrifice a little now to get the benefits later. Work hard to understand the concepts and their results.

Educate. Never stop educating yourself. Attend workshops, seminars, tutorials, vendor meetings. Keep abreast of the latest developments and how they can affect you, if not immediately, a year from now or a decade from now.

Read. Every day read something meaningful. Trade publications. Technical journals. Current events magazines. Your daily paper.

Something for pleasure. For out of reading comes a deeper understanding of it all.

These key concepts will get you a long way in a computer career. They'll give you the advantage over others that will get you the first job, the promotion, the managerial spot, or the top position. Great people in all fields have many of these qualities, so while you're young, adopt them. In this day and age, everything is wrapped up around the computer. Let the letters of this miracle machine give you a little something extra:

>COMPREHEND
>OBSERVE
>MAXIMIZE
>PROBE
>UNDERSTAND
>TRAIN
>EDUCATE
>READ

I hope *Getting into Computers* has answered most or even all of your questions. Between the many hints and suggestions within and the resources sprinkled throughout the book, you have at your fingertips the path to make the most of a career in computing.

There's but one thing left to say:

>GO OUT AND DO IT!

PART V
RESOURCES

15. PUBLICATIONS

Every field has its representative group of magazines that support various segments of that field. What sets computing apart is the incredible number of publications, their rapid proliferation, and the diverse markets or segments they reach. From highly specialized newsletters to many consumer publications, the list is virtually endless.

I have selected many publications which offer the aspiring computing person a wide overview of the industry. Some are general; some are more specific. You'll want to subscribe to or read some now as well as become aware that the others exist for future reference.

This list is by no means complete for two reasons: there are new publications arriving almost daily on the scene, and there are many too technical in nature to be included in this kind of book.

Take the time to become acquainted with these publications, for in addition to valuable news concerning computing, articles on hardware and software, features and specials, many have excellent employment classified advertising sections.

Computing now has its own TV show, *Computerworld*, meant for the general public and covering such diverse areas as computer camp for kids, computer bartending, and computerized mannequins. Produced by CW Broadcasting, it can be seen in many different cities, according to the schedule below. More cities will probably be added in the future.

Computerworld TV Schedule

Market	Station	Ch	Day	Time
New York	WOR*	9	Sat	9:30 AM
Los Angeles	KWHY	22	Sat	Noon
Chicago	WFLD	32	Sat	9:30 AM
San Francisco	KTSF	26	Sat	9:30 AM
San Jose	KSTS	48	Sun	4:30 PM
Philadelphia	WTAF	29	Tues	10:30 PM
Boston	WLVI	56	Sat	11:30 AM
Washington, DC	WBCA	20	Sat	12:00 Mid
Dallas/Ft. Worth	KNBN	33	Sat & Tues	12:30 PM & 7:30 AM
Detroit	WXON	20	Sat	10:00 AM
Houston	KHTV	39	Mon	12:00 Mid
Atlanta	WATL	36	Sat	1:30 PM
St. Louis	KDNL	30	Sun	5:30 PM

*WOR is carried on many cables around the country. Check local listings.

PUBLICATION LISTING

AEDS Monitor

Sub. Address: 1201 16th St., N.W.
Washington DC 20036
Price: free to AEDS members; others, $15/yr.
Frequency: quarterly

Scope: Timely articles on developments and directions in educational computing, both administrative and instructional. *Editorial:* news, book reviews, software reviews, applications, commentary. *Classified ads:* yes. *Recommended:* yes, if you are interested in combining education and computing.

Annals of the History of Computing

Sub. Address: AFIPS Press
1815 N. Lynn St., Suite 800
Arlington VA 22209
Price: discount to members; others, $18/yr.
Frequency: quarterly

Scope: A professional journal concerned with the history of computing and information processing. It is dedicated to the preservation and presentation of historical material, both for scholarly research and for the education of practitioners in the field. *Editorial:* news, book reviews, anecdotes, biographies, historical articles. *Classified ads:* no. *Recommended:* has interesting articles for research projects.

Byte, The Small Systems Journal

Sub. Address: Box 590
Martinsville NJ 08836
Price: $19/yr.
Frequency: monthly

Scope: The latest innovations in microcomputer technology is the emphasis of this well-known publication. *Editorial:* news, book reviews, hardware, software, and peripheral reviews, commentary, database, business news, hobby articles, calendar, games, products. *Classified ads:* yes. *Recommended:* yes.

Classroom Computer News

Sub. Address: P.O. Box 266
Cambridge MA 02138
Price: $12/yr.
Frequency: bimonthly

Scope: Profiles of important people, projects, applications, developments, and background in the field of educational computing. *Editorial:* news, software reviews, book reviews, commentary, applications, calendar, products. *Classified ads:* no. *Recommended:* highly for someone considering computing in education.

Communications News
Serving the Total Communications Market

Sub. Address: 124 S. First St.
Geneva IL 60134
Price: $18/yr.
Frequency: monthly

Scope: All that is new and noteworthy in the fields of voice, video, and data communications. *Editorial:* news, software, hardware, peripheral and book reviews, commentary, applications, hobbyist, calendar, products. *Classified ads:* yes. *Recommended:* yes, as an overall communications media.

Compute! The Journal for Progressive Computing

Sub. Address: c/o Circulation Department
P.O. Box 5406
Greensboro NC 27403
Price: $20/yr.
Frequency: monthly

Scope: Publishes programs for various microcomputers. Also insights for these owners. *Editorial:* "Overviews," reviews which combine the comments of three independent reviewers. *Classified ads:* no. *Recommended:* for people interested in programming, if your school has any of the small computers covered by this publication.

Computer Magazine

Sub. Address: IEEE Computer Society
10662 Los Vaqueros Cir.
Los Alamitos CA 90720
Price: write IEEE for details
Frequency: monthly

Scope: This is the official publication of the IEEE Computer Society, an international organization of computer scientists and engineers in all aspects of computing (see Ch. 16, Organizations). *Editorial:* events of the IEEE, educational tutorials, and general interest articles. *Recommended:* yes, if you join the IEEE.

Computer Business News
The Newsweekly for the OEM Community

Sub. Address: P.O. Box 880
Framingham MA 01701
Price: $25/yr.
Frequency: weekly

Scope: This business-oriented publication concerns itself with people already employed in all areas of computing, especially in the business aspects. *Editorial:* news, software, hardware, peripherals, commentary, business news. *Classified ads:* yes. *Recommended:* after you're in the business computing field for several years.

Computer Daily

Sub. Address: 7620 Little River Tpke.
Annandale VA 22003
Price: $750/yr.
Frequency: daily

Scope: A general interest daily newsletter, with many brief articles about what is happening in the computer industry. *Editorial:* news, hardware, software, and peripheral reviews, data-base articles, calendar, new products. *Classified ads:* no. *Recommended:* yes. See your library or computer department for possible subscriptions.

Computer Data, The Magazine for Information Management

Sub. Address: 55 Bloor St., Suite 1201
Toronto Ontario Canada M4W 3M1
Price: free to qualified people; write for additional information
Frequency: monthly

Scope: A Canadian general newsmagazine for the data-processing industry found in a variety of fields. *Editorial:* news, software and hardware reviews, commentary, business news, calendar, book reviews, new products. *Classified ads:* yes. *Recommended:* if you live in Canada and are interested in data processing.

Computer Dealer, The Magazine of Computer Marketing

Sub. Address: 20 Community Place
Morristown NJ 07960
Price: free to computer dealers
Frequency: monthly

Scope: A business-oriented magazine for third-party marketers (independent sales organizations—stores, sales groups, etc.)—selling computer products, software, and consumables. *Editorial*: news, software, hardware, and peripheral reviews, commentary, calendar, business news, case histories, new products, book reviews. *Classified ads*: yes. *Recommended*: if you are thinking about sales and marketing.

Computer Decisions, The Management Magazine of Computing

Sub. Address: 50 Essex Street
Rochelle Park NJ 07662
Price: free to computing managers
Frequency: monthly

Scope: To help those managing data centers and implementing office automation do a better job. *Editorial*: news, software, hardware, and peripheral reviews, commentary, book reviews, new products, data-base articles, applications, "round tables" on major subjects, special columns. *Classified ads*: yes. *Recommended*: yes, if you are interested in management.

Computer Design, The Magazine of Computer-Based Systems

Sub. Address: 11 Goldsmith Street
Littleton MA 01460
Price: free to digital systems engineers; others, $30/yr.
Frequency: monthly

Scope: This magazine concentrates on technological trends and developments of computer-based systems, computers, and peripheral equipment. It's a continual source of design and application ideas. *Editorial*: software and hardware articles, commentary, data-base articles, calendar, new products. *Classified ads*: yes. *Recommended*: if you are interested in computer design.

Computer/Electronic Service News, For Managers, Engineers and Technicians

Sub. Address: P.O. Box 512
Peterborough NH 03458
Price: free to qualified people; write for details
Frequency: 6 times per year

Scope: This publication brings its readers the latest developments, techniques, and strategies that can improve performance and reduce the cost of computer and electronic gear field service and maintenance. *Editorial*: business news, applications, tutorials, new products. *Classified ads*: no. *Recommended*: yes, for service-oriented people.

Computer Graphics and Applications (IEEE)

Sub. Address: IEEE Computer Society
10662 Los Vaqueros Circle
Los Alamitos CA 90720
Price: available with membership in IEEE—write for details
Frequency: quarterly

Scope: Advanced technical articles involving computer graphics, with emphasis on industrial applications, display technology, animation, methodology, computational geometry, etc. *Editorial*: feature articles, applications, new products, book reviews, calendar. *Classified ads*: no. *Recommended*: when you specialize in this area.

Computer Graphics Software News

Sub. Address: 5857 S. Gessner, Suite 401
Houston TX 77036
Price: $50/yr.
Frequency: 6 times per year

Scope: This publication features public- and private-domain software reviews dealing with computer graphics. *Editorial*: news, applications, calendar, software reviews, new products. *Classified ads*: no. *Recommended*: for students specializing in computer graphics.

Computer Graphics World

Sub. Address: 54 Mint Street
San Francisco CA 94103
Price: $25/yr.
Frequency: monthly

Scope: This magazine features application-oriented articles from the user's point of view, on such topics as computer-aided design, automated cartography, image processing, and business graphics. *Editorial*: feature articles, new products and services, "Newsfront," book reviews, columns. *Recommended*: to students specializing in computer graphics.

Computer Industry Marketing Newsletter

Sub. Address: 10100 Old River Rd.
Forestville CA 95436
Price: $60/yr.
Frequency: monthly

Scope: A timely, monthly newsletter restricted in content to developments, research, observation, and background of value to those involved in computer marketing, advertising, and sales. *Editorial:* "end-user buying behavior statistical profile" study, projections, news, franchising, regulations, new products, techniques, etc. *Recommended:* yes.

Computer Literature Index

Sub. Address: P.O. Box 9280
Phoenix AZ 85068
Price: $75/yr.
Frequency: quarterly

Scope: This is an abstracting and indexing service, by subject and author, of current computer literature, which can be found in libraries. It consists of abstracts of books, periodicals, conference reports, etc. *Recommended:* for use in research involving most any sector of computing.

Computer Marketing Newsletter

Sub. Address: 1000 Quail, Suite 120
Newport Beach CA 92660
Price: $72/yr.
Frequency: monthly

Scope: This is the original publication devoted to computer industry sales and marketing news. *Editorial:* news, commentary, helpful articles, sales compensation, book reviews. *Classified ads:* career and business opportunity listings for subscribers only. *Recommended:* for those interested in selling and marketing.

Computer Merchandising, The Magazine for High Technology Retailers

Sub. Address: 15720 Ventura Blvd., Suite 610
Encino CA 91436
Price: free to qualified people; others, $18/yr.
Frequency: monthly

Scope: The goal of this publication is to promote successful merchandising techniques and sales effectiveness at all levels of computer retailing, using retailers as the basis for articles. *Editorial:* news, book reviews, commentary, business news, applications, calendar, games, new products. *Classified ads:* no. *Recommended:* for those students considering retail sales of computers.

Computer Music Journal

Sub. Address: Journals Dept., The MIT Press
28 Carleton Street
Cambridge MA 02142
Price: $20/yr.
Frequency: quarterly

Scope: This university-produced journal covers research and developments in computer-generated music and digital audio. *Editorial:* software, hardware, and peripheral reviews, news, book reviews, commentary, calendar, new products. *Classified ads:* no. *Recommended:* a specialized journal for those interested in this specialty.

Computer Retailing

Sub. Address: 760 Peachtree Road
Atlanta GA 30357
Price: free to qualified trade; write for details
Frequency: monthly

Scope: A trade publication for retailers of microcomputers and small-business computer systems. *Editorial:* news, software reviews, business news, applications, commentary, games, new products. *Classified ads:* no. *Recommended:* for students considering a career in a retail computer store.

Computer Sales Digest

Sub. Address: 4954 William Arnold Road
Memphis TN 38117
Price: $95/yr.
Frequency: monthly

Scope: A source of computer industry marketing and sales aids and services aimed at increasing sales of computers and computer related products. *Editorial:* news, techniques, strategies, how-tos, case histories, marketplace. *Classified ads:* no. *Recommended:* for sales-oriented students.

Computers in Hospitals

Sub. Address: 3900 S. Wadsworth Blvd., Suite 560
Denver CO 80235
Price: $10.95/yr.
Frequency: 6 times per year

Scope: A magazine focusing exclusively on developments, applications, news, and technology for computer uses in hospitals. *Editorial:*

news, contracts, new products, regulatory news, features, profiles, columns, calendar. *Classified ads:* yes. *Recommended:* for students combining medicine and computers.

Computers in Psychiatry/Psychology

Sub. Address: 26 Trumbull Street
New Haven CT 06511
Price: $25/yr.
Frequency: 6 times per year

Scope: A publication for professionals interested in the use of computers in psychiatry and clinical psychology and related areas. *Editorial:* software reviews, book reviews, applications, commentary, data-base articles, new products. *Classified ads:* yes. *Recommended:* for students looking into this specialty.

COMPUTERWORLD, *The Newsweekly for the Computer Community*

Sub. Address: 375 Cochituate Road
Framingham MA 01701
Price: $36/yr.
Frequency: weekly

Scope: This is the "bible" of the computer community, with extensive news and in-depth treatment of a wide range of topics. This publication is published by CW Communications, the same company that has started the TV show previously discussed. *Editorial:* features, news, software, hardware, peripherals, communications, systems. *Classified ads:* excellent career classified section. *Recommended:* highly.

Computing Teacher, The

Sub. Address: Computer and Information Science Department
University of Oregon
Eugene OR 97403
Price: $14.50/yr.
Frequency: 9 issues per year

Scope: This university-produced publication emphasizes teaching about computers, using computers for instruction and staff support, teacher education, and the impact of computers on the curriculum. *Editorial:* news, book reviews, software reviews, commentary, calendar, think pieces, features. *Classified ads:* yes. *Recommended:* for students interested in educational computing.

Creative Computing

Sub. Address: 39 East Hanover Avenue
Morris Plains NJ 07950
Price: $20/yr.
Frequency: monthly

Scope: This leading magazine of computer applications and software provides unbiased information to those people considering purchasing hardware and software. *Editorial:* news, software, hardware, and peripheral reviews, commentary, book reviews, business news, calendar, applications, games, new products. *Classified ads:* no. *Recommended:* yes, for microcomputer students.

Datamation

Sub. Address: 1301 S. Grove Avenue
Barrington IL 60010
Price: free to qualified people; write for details
Frequency: 13 times per year

Scope: A publication for data-processing professionals covering a wide spectrum of topics in the electronic data-processing (EDP) marketplace. *Editorial:* software, hardware, career marketplace, trade show coverage, salary surveys, special issues. *Classified ads:* yes. *Recommended:* if you are interested in data processing.

Dental Computer Newsletter

Sub. Address: 1000 North Avenue
Waukegan IL 60085
Price: $15/yr.
Frequency: monthly

Scope: This publication concerns itself with microcomputers and minisystems which can be used by the physician or dentist in their professions to better handle their specific workloads. *Editorial:* news, software, hardware, and peripheral reviews, book reviews, commentary, business news, applications, new products, hobbyist. *Classified ads:* yes. *Recommended:* for students combining computing and medicine.

Desktop Computing

Sub. Address: P.O. Box 917
Farmingdale NY 11737
Price: $25/yr.
Frequency: monthly

Scope: A computer magazine written in "plain English," geared toward users of computers in business settings. *Editorial:* news, software, hardware, and peripheral reviews, commentary, data-base articles, business news, applications, case histories. *Classified ads:* no. *Recommended:* yes.

Digital Design, Computers • Peripherals • Systems

Sub. Address: 1050 Commonwealth Avenue
Boston MA 02215
Price: free to qualified people; others, $35/yr.
Frequency: monthly

Scope: A technical magazine circulated to research, development and design engineers, covering topics appropriate to these people and relating to the development of computing systems. *Editorial:* trends, special reports, features, hardware, software, peripherals, new products. *Classified ads:* yes. *Recommended:* to those pursuing the design area.

Dr. Dobb's Journal, For Users of Small Computer Systems

Sub. Address: P.O. Box E
Menlo Park CA 94025
Price: $25/yr.
Frequency: monthly

Scope: This is a magazine devoted to software and systems design, telecommunications, programming tips and listings, and language development. *Editorial:* news, software, hardware, and peripheral reviews, applications, book reviews, commentary, calendar, new products, games. *Classified ads:* yes. *Recommended:* for programming students.

EDP Performance Review
The Monthly Report on EDP Performance Improvement

Sub. Address: P.O. Box 9280
Phoenix AZ 85068
Price: $60/yr.
Frequency: monthly

Scope: This newsletter discusses the improvement of data-processing operations, development, and planning, with emphasis on new approaches to managing and controlling human and machine resources. *Editorial:* tutorials, book reviews, calendar, new products. *Classified ads:* no. *Recommended:* if you are interested in the operations aspect of data processing.

EDP Weekly

Sub. Address: 7620 Little River Tpke.
Annandale VA 22003
Price: $120/yr.
Frequency: weekly

Scope: General news of the computer/communications industry and some analysis of specific areas. *Editorial:* news, software, hardware, and peripheral reviews, data-base articles, business news, applications, book reviews, new products, calendar. *Classified ads:* no. *Recommended:* yes, for students of data processing.

Educational Computer Magazine
Educating Tomorrow's Computer Users

Sub. Address: P.O. Box 535
Cupertino CA
Price: $18/yr.
Frequency: bimonthly

Scope: A new publication aimed at the educational computer marketplace. *Editorial:* news, book reviews, software, hardware, and peripheral reviews, commentary, data-base articles, applications, calendar, new products. *Classified ads:* no. *Recommended:* not available for review at press time.

The Futurist
A Journal of Forecasts, Trends, and Ideas about the Future

Sub. Address: 4916 St. Elmo Ave.
Bethesda MD 20814
Price: $20/yr.
Frequency: bimonthly

Scope: This publication focuses on trends and developments that are likely to have a major impact on the way we will live in the years ahead. *Editorial:* news, articles reflecting the authors' views. *Classified ads:* yes. *Recommended:* perhaps for reading about the future of computing when it is covered in the publication.

EFTS Industry Report

Sub. Address: 7620 Little River Tpke.
Annandale VA 22003
Price: $88/yr.
Frequency: periodic

Scope: This newsletter covers the field of electronic funds transfer (EFTS) which includes electronic money, cashless society, point of sale, and related legislation. *Editorial:* news, new products, reviews, commentary. *Classified ads:* no. *Recommended:* if you are interested in the financial area combining computing and money.

Genealogical Computing

Sub. Address: 5102 Pommeroy Drive
Fairfax VA 22032
Price: $12/yr.
Frequency: bimonthly

Scope: This highly specialized publication focuses on genealogical uses of personal computers. *Editorial:* news, software reviews, commentary, data-base articles, applications. *Classified ads:* yes. *Recommended:* more as a hobby area than a career path.

Graduating Engineer
Bringing Industry into the Classroom

Sub. Address: McGraw Hill Publications Company, Rm. 345
1221 Avenue of the Americas
New York NY 10020
Price: free to senior-level engineering and computer science students
Frequency: 4 times during academic year

Scope: This publication is a must for those computer students studying for design, hardware, and other technical positions. *Editorial:* employment education articles are directed toward the initial career needs of seniors. *Classified ads:* no. *Recommended:* very highly.

High Technology, For Managers Who Have to Know

Sub. Address: P.O. Box 2810
Boulder CO 80322
Price: $12/yr.
Frequency: bimonthly

Scope: This upper-level magazine provides essential input for corporate managers, planners, and decision-makers who must know what is happening on the leading edge of technology. *Editorial:* news, book reviews, business news, applications, commentary. *Classified ads:* no. *Recommended:* good reading for students interested in management.

Home and Educational Computing!

Sub. Address: P.O. Box 5406
Greensboro NC 27403
Price: $12/yr.
Frequency: bimonthly

Scope: This publication provides telecommunications, applications, and tutorial articles on the new smaller computers, with programs and hints for the use of computers in education and as terminals in the home. *Classified ads*: no. *Recommended*: yes, for programming students and those interested in educational computing.

Infosystems, The Information Systems Magazine for Management

Sub. Address: Hitchcock Building
Wheaton IL 60187
Price: free to qualified people; others, $40/yr.
Frequency: monthly

Scope: This publication aims at management concerned with a variety of subjects involving information systems—computers, software, personnel management, word processing, etc. *Editorial*: news, hardware, software, and peripheral reviews, commentary, book reviews, data-base articles, business news, applications, calendar, new products. *Classified ads*: yes. *Recommended*: for management students.

Infoworld

Sub. Address: CW Communications
P.O. Box 880
Framingham MA 01701
Price: free to qualified people; others, $25/yr.
Frequency: weekly

Scope: This is a magazine for the microcomputer user who wants to keep abreast of new developments in products, services, applications, and technological trends. *Editorial*: news, software, and hardware reviews, book reviews, commentary, calendar, new products. *Classified ads*: yes. *Recommended*: yes, a good general newspaper for students to become familiar with.

Interactive Computing
The Journal of the Association of Computer Users

Sub. Address: P.O. Box 9003
Boulder CO 80301
Price: write for details
Frequency: every other month

Scope: A *Consumer Reports* type of publication accepting no advertising and analyzing computer products. Recognized is their "Benchmark Reports" covering a wide range of computers. *Recommended:* yes, especially when you buy a personal computer for yourself.

Interface Age, Computing for Business and Home

Sub. Address: 16704 Marquardt Avenue
Cerritos CA 90701
Price: $18/yr.
Frequency: monthly

Scope: This publication covers microcomputing in business and consumer electronics, keeping abreast of the latest technologies, breakthroughs, and applications. *Editorial:* software, hardware, and peripheral reviews, commentary, book reviews, data-base articles, business articles, calendar, new products. *Classified ads:* yes. *Recommended:* yes.

Journal of Micrographics

Sub. Address: 8719 Colesville Rd.
Silver Spring MD 20910
Price: $55 to nonmembers of NMA
Frequency: monthly

Scope: This publication is devoted to the science, technology, art, applications, and products of micrographics and other information management technologies. *Editorial:* news, features, new products, reviews, applications, etc. *Recommended:* this is a highly specialized area, not requiring utilizing this publication while in school.

Microcomputing

Sub. Address: P.O. Box 997
Farmingdale NY 11737
Price: $25/yr.
Frequency: monthly

Scope: Here you will find information on all types of microcomputers and software, slightly technical but interesting and informative to the beginner as well as the professional computer user. *Editorial:* software, hardware, and peripheral reviews, commentary, book reviews, data-base articles, applications, hobbyist, calendar, games, new products. *Classified ads:* yes. *Recommended:* yes, as an excellent "get acquainted" publication.

MAN Society Technology
Journal of the American Industrial Arts Association

Sub. Address: 1914 Association Drive
Reston VA 22091
Price: $20/yr.
Frequency: 8 times per year

Scope: A technologically-oriented journal dedicated to industrial arts, and how that field is affected by the new technology. *Editorial:* news, hardware, software, and peripheral reviews, commentary, applications, new products, calendar. *Classified ads:* yes. *Recommended:* yes.

MICRO (IEEE)

Sub. Address: IEEE Computer Society
10662 Los Vaqueros Circle
Los Alamitos CA 90720
Price: write IEEE for details
Frequency: quarterly

Scope: This is a microcomputing magazine for the professional hardware and software engineer, covering appropriate topics. *Editorial:* applications, features, new products, calendar. *Recommended:* for computer engineering students.

Micro, The 6502/6809 Journal

Sub. Address: 34 Chelmsford Street
Chelmsford MA 01824
Price: $18/yr.
Frequency: monthly

Scope: This magazine is for users of specific microcomputers who want to learn about their computers' inner workings, and who want to keep up with high-level language developments. *Editorial:* software and hardware listings, book listings, applications, commentary. *Classified ads:* yes. *Recommended:* yes.

Microcomputers in Education
The Journal of Educational Software

Sub. Address: 5 Chapel Hill Drive
Fairfield CT 06433
Price: $24/yr.
Frequency: monthly

Scope: This publication specializes in educational software and related products and events. *Editorial:* news, software reviews, book re-

views, commentary, calendar, new products. *Classified ads:* yes.
Recommended: for those interested in education and computing.

Microcomputing Industry

Sub. Address: Elm Street
Peterborough NH 03458
Price: free to qualified people and companies; write for details
Frequency: monthly

Scope: An industry newsletter, giving information on happenings within the microcomputing industry—new developments, personnel changes, mergers, etc. *Editorial:* news, book reviews, commentary, calendar, new products. *Classified ads:* no. *Recommended:* yes.

Microscope

Sub. Address: P.O. Box 1700
University of Victoria
Victoria British Columbia Canada V8W 2Y2
Price: $12/yr.
Frequency: 5 times per year

Scope: This university-produced magazine is for teachers and students using microcomputers. *Editorial:* news, book reviews, software, hardware, and peripheral reviews, commentary. *Classified ads:* yes. *Recommended:* yes, especially while in school.

Microsystems, The CP/M and S-100 User's Journal

Sub. Address: 39 East Hanover Ave.
Morris Plains NJ 07950
Price: $10/yr.
Frequency: 6 times per year

Scope: This publication is for the more sophisticated user and designer (both software and hardware) of microcomputer systems, particularly those using the CP/M- and S-100-based hardware systems. *Editorial:* news, software, hardware, and peripheral reviews, commentary, book reviews, data-base articles, applications, new products, tutorials. *Classified ads:* yes. *Recommended:* for students specializing in designing.

National Report on Computers and Health

Sub. Address: 5010-I Nicholson Lane
Rockville MD 20852
Price: $192/yr.
Frequency: biweekly

Scope: This professional report addresses itself to issues, trends, and developments of importance to health care and information-processing professionals. *Editorial:* news, book reviews, commentary, business news, applications, calendar, new products, organizations. *Classified ads:* no. *Recommended:* if you plan to combine computing and health care.

OCR *Today*

Sub. Address: 10 Banta Place
Hackensack NJ 07601
Price: $10/yr.
Frequency: quarterly

Scope: This is the official publication of the Optical Character Recognition Users Association, presenting articles dealing with this specialized field. *Editorial:* features, calendar, new products, reviews, people, tutorials. *Classified ads:* no. *Recommended:* yes, if you are interested in optical character recognition.

The Office, *Magazine of Management* • *Equipment* • *Automation*

Sub. Address: 1200 Summer Street
Stamford CT 06904
Price: $25/yr.
Frequency: monthly

Scope: This publication presents articles and applications that will assist administrative, data-processing, records-management, word-processing, and office executives in improving their paperwork and data-handling operations. *Editorial:* news, software reviews, book reviews, commentary, data-base articles, business news, applications, new products. *Classified ads:* no. *Recommended:* yes, if any of the above areas interest you.

Online

Sub. Address: 11 Tannery Lane
Weston CT 06883
Price: $78/yr.
Frequency: bimonthly

Scope: This magazine is edited primarily for information managers, librarians, and others who make use of commercially available on-line bibliographic services. A practical, how-to journal that covers the on-line industry in a broad way. *Editorial:* news, commentary, data-base articles, business news. *Classified ads:* yes. *Recommended:* for students of data-base theory.

Parity

Sub. Address: 1000 Connecticut Ave., N.W., Suite 9
Washington DC 20036
Price: $15/yr.
Frequency: quarterly

Scope: A career-oriented publication for those people in the area of information processing. *Editorial*: data-base articles, book reviews, applications, new products, calendar. *Classified ads*: yes. *Recommended*: yes.

Pergamon Computer Journals

Sub. Address: Fairview Park
Elmsford NY 10523
Price: write for details
Frequency: write for details

This international company puts out a group of technical journals, some of which are about computers and electrical engineering, fluids, chemical engineering, chemistry, graphics, etc. Write for their catalogue, which describes each journal in detail. *Recommended*: check your library—they're good for advanced studies and research.

Peripherals Digest

Sub. Address: 7620 Little River Tpke.
Annandale VA 22003
Price: $88/yr.
Frequency: periodic

Scope: A digest of computer peripherals, their markets and the industry as a whole. *Editorial*: book reviews, hardware and peripheral reviews, business news, calendar, new products. *Classified ads*: no. *Recommended*: yes, once in the field specializing in peripherals.

Personal Computer Letter

Sub. Address: 174 Concord St., Suite 23
Peterborough NH 03458
Price: $200/yr.
Frequency: monthly

Scope: This personal newsletter carries new ideas, analyses, and professional-quality research that you would have trouble finding elsewhere, written to give its audience independent analyses and opinions. No advertising. *Editorial*: features. *Recommended*: ask for a sample issue as a student and see if it is worthwhile; also, an editorial calendar is available.

Personal Computing Magazine

Sub. Address: P.O. Box 13916
Philadelphia PA 19101
Price: $24/yr.
Frequency: monthly

Scope: A general interest publication focusing on the personal aspect of small computers and their applications. *Editorial:* features, hardware and software reviews, calendar, book reviews, educational computing. *Classified ads:* yes. *Recommended:* yes.

Physician's Desktop Computer Letter

Sub. Address: 10367 Paw Paw Lake Drive
Mattawan MI 49071
Price: $72/yr.
Frequency: 11 issues per year

Scope: This specialized newsletter provides the physician and staff with up-to-date information and tutorials on the application of desktop computer hardware and software in clinics and general practice. *Editorial:* hardware, software, and peripheral reviews, applications, new products. *Classified ads:* no. *Recommended:* yes, if you have an interest in combining computing with the medical field.

Popular Computing, The Key to Understanding

Sub. Address: P.O. Box 307
Martinsville NJ 08836
Price: $15/yr.
Frequency: monthly

Scope: This publication is aimed at the nontechnical reader (business people, educators, managers, etc.) who want to learn about computing in an easy-to-understand manner. *Editorial:* news, hardware, software, and peripheral reviews, book reviews, commentary, database articles, business news, applications, hobbyist, calendar, new products, games. *Classified ads:* yes. *Recommended:* good introductory publication for computer students.

PRIVACY JOURNAL
An Independent Monthly on Privacy in a Computer Age

Sub. Address: P.O. Box 8844
Washington DC 20003
Price: $65/yr.
Frequency: monthly

Scope: This publication seeks to support Americans' right to privacy as outlined in the Fourth Amendment, providing information about surveillance, rights to records on health, credit, employment, insurance, computer security, and legislation affecting privacy. This issue will grow as computers proliferate. *Editorial:* news, book reviews, commentary, business news. *Classified ads:* no. *Recommended:* good source for an unusual term paper; good nonrequired reading.

Scientific Laboratory Computer Letter

Sub. Address: 10367 Paw Paw Lake Drive
Mattawan MI 49071
Price: $54/yr.
Frequency: 11 issues per year

Scope: This publication provides the scientist and manager with up-to-date information and tutorials on the application of desktop computer hardware and software in the laboratory setting. *Editorial:* software, hardware, and peripheral reviews, applications, new products. *Classified ads:* no. *Recommended:* this newsletter good for science-oriented computing students.

Small Business Computers Magazine

Sub. Address: P.O. Box 789-M
Morristown NJ 07960
Price: $12/yr.
Frequency: 6 times per year

Scope: This publication addresses itself to business people who purchase small computers, for use in departments of large firms or in small companies. *Editorial:* news, book reviews, software, hardware, and peripheral reviews, commentary, data-base articles, business news, applications, calendar, new products. *Classified ads:* yes. *Recommended:* for the student interested in the business aspect of computing.

Software Digest

Sub. Address: 7620 Little River Tpke.
Annandale VA 22003
Price: $88/yr.
Frequency: periodical

Scope: This newsletter is a comprehensive digest of the software markets and all that is available to the end-users. *Editorial:* software reviews, data-base articles, business news, applications, calendar, new products. *Classified ads:* no. *Recommended:* for software-oriented students.

Software News, The Computer Software Products Newspaper

Sub. Address: 5 Kane Industrial Drive
Hudson MA 01749
Price: free to qualified people
Frequency: monthly

Scope: This publication carries news of interest to people who buy, specify, or develop software. *Editorial:* news, software reviews, book reviews, commentary, data-base articles, business news, applications, calendar, new products. *Classified ads:* yes. *Recommended:* to students specializing in software.

Technoartistry, Taking Creativity into the Twenty-first Century

Sub. Address: 4 Meadowood Ct.
Huntington NY 11743
Price: $50/yr.
Frequency: periodic

Scope: This newsletter covers the application of current technology in the graphic arts field. *Editorial:* news, software and hardware reviews, commentary, applications, how-tos. *Classified ads:* no. *Recommended:* for students combining graphic arts and computing.

Technological Horizons in Education, T.H.E. Journal

Sub. Address: P.O. Box 992
Acton MA 01720
Price: free to qualified educators
Frequency: 6 times per year.

Scope: This magazine addresses itself to technology and its uses in education, industry training, government, hospitals, and businesses. *Editorial:* news, book reviews, software, hardware, peripherals, commentary, applications, calendar, new products. *Classified ads:* yes. *Recommended:* yes.

Technology Illustrated, For Educated Consumers Who Want to Know

Sub. Address: P.O. Box 2806
Boulder CO 80322
Price: $9.95/yr.
Frequency: monthly in 1983

Scope: This magazine is for educated and literate people who are curious about the technologies that surround them but are untrained in science or engineering. *Editorial:* software, hardware, and peripheral reviews, book reviews, commentary, business news, applications, hobbyist, games, new products. *Classified ads:* no. *Recommended:* as an easy reading introduction to many different areas.

Word Processing and Information Systems
The Magazine of Automated Business Communications

Sub. Address: 51 Madison Avenue
New York NY 10010
Price: $16/yr.
Frequency: monthly

Scope: This publication covers, in depth, the word-processing and information systems sectors of the computing industry, with a lot of practical, usable information. *Editorial:* features, supervisory overviews, case histories, training, career paths, trends, forecasts, columns, calendar. *Recommended:* yes, for word-/information-processing students.

16. ORGANIZATIONS

Every industry or field is supported in numerous ways through organizations which seek to further that industry. Usually nonprofit, these organizations either represent a specific group of companies or people or address themselves to specific issues.

You'll find in this chapter an extensive listing of computer-oriented organizations, with a brief description of their purpose and information on membership, student chapters, publications, etc.

Most of these organizations have brochures that are free for the asking. Some have career information, and those offering student chapters should be immediately contacted if your interest is in the area addressed by that organization.

I have taken the liberty to "recommend" contacting certain organizations, but that doesn't mean you shouldn't contact the others. Many of these organizations conduct seminars or tutorials to enhance one's skills; being active in these groups during the length of your employment is generally a wise thing to do.

ORGANIZATION LISTING

American Federation of Information Processing Societies (AFIPS)

1815 North Lynn Street
Arlington VA 22209
(703) 558-3600

Purpose: Providing an umbrella structure in which other organizations with a primary interest in information processing could join together to advance the arts and sciences of this field. *Membership:* composed of 11 national organizations, with a total of over 135,000 members. *Events sponsored:* National Computer Conference, Office Automation Conference. *Publications:* Conference Proceedings, Annals of the History of Computing, AFIPS Press Catalog, Headquarters Newsletters, Washington Report, Washington Calendar. *Career information:* yes. *Student chapters:* many of the 11 constituent members have student chapters. *Recommended:* yes.

American Society for Information Science (ASIS)

1010 Sixteenth Street, N.W.
Washington DC 20036
(202) 659-3644

Purpose: A nonprofit professional organization designed for scientific, literary, and educational purposes, dedicated to the creation, organization, dissemination, and application of knowledge concerning information and its transfer. *Membership*: regular ($55), student ($15), or institutional available. *Events sponsored*: annual meeting, 23 special interest groups for technical subjects. *Publications*: Journal of the American Society for Information Science, Bulletin, ASIS News, Annual Review of Information Science and Technology, Proceedings, Computer-Readable Data Bases, ASIS Handbook and Directory. *Career information*: yes; operates placement service with "jobline." *Student chapters*: 24 chapters have been chartered nationwide. *Recommended*: highly.

Association for Computers and the Humanities (ACH)

Queens College
Flushing NY 11367

Purpose: To foster and exchange information on computer applications in humanistic scholarship. *Membership*: about 300 members, chiefly academics; $15 per year. *Events sponsored*: International Conference on Computers and the Humanities (biennial), technical programs as part of the Modern Language Association's annual meetings. *Publications*: ACH Newsletter. *Student chapters*: not at this time. *Recommended*: if specialty is in this area.

Association for Computing Machinery (ACM)

1133 Avenue of the Americas
New York NY 10036
(212) 265-6300

Purpose: A worldwide educational and scientific organization, the ACM serves to advance the sciences and arts of information processing, promote the interchange of information, and to develop and maintain the integrity and competence of individuals engaged in information processing. *Membership*: over 50,000 members; member or associate member ($40.00) or student member ($13.00). *Events sponsored*: 100 regular chapters, over 30 special interest groups, Annual Conference, Computer Science Conference, National Computer Conference. *Publications*: Communications of the ACM, Computing Practices, Communications, Journal of the ACM, Computing Reviews, Computing Surveys, and several Transaction publications, plus special publications. *Career information*: yes. *Student chapters*: 255 chapters now in existence with conferences and competitions. *Recommended*: highly.

Association for Educational Data Systems (AEDS)

1201 Sixteenth Street, N.W.
Washington DC 20036
(202) 833-4100

Purpose: To provide an arena for educational professionals engaged in the development and implementation of technology in school systems at all levels, for interchange of information and ideas. *Membership:* 2,200 education personnel on various levels; individual ($35.00), student ($10.00), and company/institutional available. *Events sponsored:* AEDS Workshops, annual convention, sponsors the AEDS Computer Programming Contest for students in grades 7–12; 21 geographic affiliates. *Publications:* AEDS Monitor, AEDS Journal, proceedings. *Student chapters:* not at this time. *Recommended:* when you choose a specialty in computer education, you should consider joining AEDS.

Association for Systems Management (ASM)

24587 Bagley Road
Cleveland OH 44138
(216) 243-6900

Purpose: International professional organization dedicated to the advancement of systems analysts and managers, to provide for continuing education needs of the systems practitioner. *Membership:* there are 9,500 members, broken down into 125 chapters and 21 division councils; experience or degree required for membership; student memberships available. *Events sponsored:* week-long education courses, seminars, annual conference. *Publications:* Journal of Systems Management, systems books. *Recommended:* once a specialty in systems has been chosen, the ASM is recommended.

Association of Computer Programmers and Analysts (ACPA)

11800 Sunrise Valley Drive, Suite 808
Reston VA 22091
(703) 476-5437

Purpose: To provide educational opportunities to develop professional skills, career guidance, contact and taking an active role in the futuring of the data- and information-processing fields. *Membership:* regular ($35.00), student ($10.00—open to students starting at the high school level), and others available; chapters throughout the U.S. *Events sponsored:* professional seminars, annual conference. *Publications:* THRUPUT, an international newsletter, ACPA technical papers, chapter newsletters. *Career information:* yes. *Recommended:* yes.

Organizations

Association of Computer Users (ACU)

P.O. Box 9003
Boulder CO 80301
(303) 443-3600

Purpose: A nonprofit organization in a totally independent mode acting as an information clearinghouse and nonpartisan evaluation of current computer technology. *Membership:* several thousand worldwide; membership ($60.00) includes "section" membership in a specialty area. *Publications:* ACU Bulletin, Interactive Computing, Benchmark Reports, series of newsletters for each section area. *Career information:* not, at press, employed.

Association of Data Processing Service Organizations (ADAPSO)

1300 North 17th Street, Suite 300
Arlington VA 22209
(703) 522-5055

Purpose: A trade association representing computer services firms, to keep membership informed on issues relating to the industry and aid member firms in areas of taxation, contracts, compensation, research, etc. *Membership:* under 500 firms, with no personal memberships available. *Events sponsored:* seminar programs, management conferences, financial analysts meeting. *Career information:* not available at this time. *Student chapters:* none. *Recommended:* after hiring, see if your firm is a member; take advantage of the services offered if your company is a member.

Association of Rehabilitation Programs in Data Processing (ARPDP)

c/o Michigan State Technical Institute and Rehabilitation Center
Alber Drive
Plainwell MI 49080

Purpose: This is an international nonprofit educational association, its goals being to promote communications between programs designed to train handicapped people in the skills of data processing. *Membership:* consists of data-processing personnel and rehabilitation specialists who have either been involved or are involved in the training programs. *Publications:* Viewpoint. *Recommended:* yes, if you are interested in combining computing and working with disabled persons.

Association for Women in Computing (AWC)

407 Hillmoor Drive
Silver Spring MD 20901

Purpose: This organization was founded to promote communication among women in computing, further the professional advancement and development and to promote the education of women of all ages in computer technology. *Membership:* $15 per year; student, $5.00. *Events sponsored:* meetings at computer conferences. *Publications:* AWC Newsletter. *Recommended:* yes, for all women seeking a career in computing.

Canadian Information Processing Society (CIPS)

243 College Street, 5th Floor
Toronto Ontario Canada M5T 2Y1
(416) 593-4040

Purpose: The largest computer association in Canada, CIPS was formed to advance computer and information processing through education, publishing and other means. *Membership:* More than 4,000 members with special interest groups and local sections. Fees vary depending on location from $100; students from $57.00. *Events sponsored:* conferences, meetings, etc. *Publications:* CIPS Review, Canadian Computer Census; students receive INFOR Journal. *Career information:* yes. *Recommended:* yes.

CAUSE

737 29th Street
Boulder CO 80303
(303) 449-4430

Purpose: CAUSE is the professional association for individuals engaged in the development, use, and management of information systems in higher education. Keeps membership informed of rapidly changing trends, national issues, and exchange of information. *Membership:* 1,300 members on 550 college campuses; fees based on college size. *Events sponsored:* National Conference, Information Exchange Library, Information Request Service, Consulting Service. *Publications:* CAUSE/EFFECT Magazine, newsletter, monographs, directory, conference proceedings. *Recommended:* once in the field, an important organization.

Center for Computer Law

P.O. Box 54308 T.A.
Los Angeles CA 90054
(213) 748-9416

Purpose: To promote the orderly development of the law as it applies to the computer, telecommunications, and information industries, through publications, research and education. *Membership*: $25.00 individual, $100.00 for corporation. *Events sponsored*: special projects, major library. *Publications*: computer/law journal, monograph series, books, 3 special projects in process. *Recommended*: yes, as a valuable source of up-to-date information.

Computer and Automated Systems Association of SME (CASA/SME)

1 SME Drive
Dearborn MI 48128
(313) 271-1500

Purpose: This organization, a division of the Society of Manufacturing Engineers, was formed to provide comprehensive coverage of the field of computers and automation in the advancement of manufacturing. It is designed to bring together aspects of manufacturing involving computers in an educational and professional manner. *Membership*: Over 5,000 individuals who work in the field are members; annual dues are $35.00 plus a $15.00 initiation. *Events sponsored*: local chapters, technical council, educational programs, employment assistance, and certification program. *Publications*: Manufacturing Engineering, newsletters, reference books. *Career information*: yes; members can get listing in magazine free of charge; employment tips publication. *Recommended*: once in the field.

Computer Law Association, Inc.

c/o Daniel T. Brooks, Secretary
6106 Lorcom Ct.
Springfield VA 22152

Purpose: This organization is for lawyers concerned with the legal problems arising from the invention, evolution, production, marketing, acquisition, and use of computer communications technology. *Membership*: mainly attorneys and law students; $25.00 per year; students $5.00. *Events sponsored*: semiannual meetings. *Publications*: transcripts of proceedings at the association's semiannual meetings. *Recommended*: the field of computer law is a growing one, and for someone interested in this aspect, yes.

Data Entry Management Association (DEMA)

P.O. Box 3231
Stamford CT 06905
(203) 322-1166

Purpose: This is an international educational association, designed to promote the professional growth and enhance the prestige of men and women responsible for capturing data for the computer. *Membership:* there are several major and local chapters; annual fee is $55.00. *Events sponsored:* annual conference, equipment exhibit, workshops, miniconferences, seminars. *Publications:* DEMA newsletter, surveys, books; operates reference library, and advisory service in solving personnel and technical problems and in providing information. *Recommended:* once in the field.

Data Processing Management Association (DPMA)

505 Busse Highway
Park Ridge IL 60068
(312) 693-5070

Purpose: The largest organization serving the information and computer management community, the DPMA engages in education and research activities focused on programs for the self-improvement of its members. *Membership:* managerial or supervisory data-processing personnel; systems and methods analysts; data-processing educators; holders of the Certificate in Data Processing. *Events sponsored:* a major program is the certification one, designed to establish high standards based on a broad educational framework. *Publications:* Data Management Magazine; write for additional information. *Recommended:* for data processing people, yes.

EDUCOM

P.O. Box 364
Princeton NJ 08540
(609) 734-1915

Purpose: This is a consortium of over 350 colleges and universities and other institutions associated with higher education. It was founded in 1964 to promote cooperative efforts in the application of computing and information technology in higher education. While membership is on the collegiate vs. individual level, one can benefit if he or she is interested in computing and higher education. *Events sponsored:* annual conference, seminars, workshops. *Publications:* EDUCOM bulletin, quarterly magazine, monographs, conference proceedings; operates special network and consulting group. *Student chapters:* no. *Recommended:* if combining higher education and computing, then check into your college to see if they belong.

The Foundation for the Advancement of Computer-aided Education

20863 Stevens Creek Blvd.
Building B-2, Suite A-1
Cupertino CA 95014

Purpose: This foundation is a national, nonprofit corporation established to support and develop new methods of learning through the use of small computers. The foundation directs its resources to organizations and individuals for projects aimed at creating innovative methods of learning through low cost technology. It awards grants for projects deemed appropriate with the foundations' philosophy. *Publications:* Journals of Courseware Review. *Recommended:* if your interest is educational computing, yes; write for application procedures and evaluation methods.

Government Management Information Sciences (GMIS)

c/o R.M. Hackett
City Water Board
Box 2449
San Antonio TX 78298

Purpose: This organization of local governments fosters the sharing of information and ideas in the utilization of computer technology in local governments. *Membership:* about 150 local governments and agencies; it focuses solely on the data-processing needs of local governments. *Events sponsored:* international conference. *Publications:* GEM Newsletter, annual survey of member data processing installations. *Career information:* while not published, people involved in GMIS can discuss careers in government data processing and provide valuable insight. *Recommended:* investigate further if your interest lies in government computing.

IEEE Computer Society

1109 Spring Street, Suite 201
Silver Spring, MD 20910
(301) 589-3386

Purpose: This major organization was formed to pursue the goals of the computer sciences through education, research, and sharing of information. *Membership:* over 52,000 individuals, worldwide; write for membership information. *Events sponsored:* more than 40 conferences and workshops every year. *Publications:* the IEEE Computer Society is the world's largest publisher of computer proceedings. *Career information:* yes. *Student chapters:* yes. *Recommended:* highly.

Independent Computer Consultants Association

P.O. Box 27412
St. Louis MO 63141
(314) 567-9708

Purpose: This organization promotes professionalism within the data-processing industry. *Membership:* over 600 individuals or companies who provide computer products or services belong; fees are $84.00 national; local dues are set by the city involved. *Events sponsored:* annual conference—exchange of ideas. *Publications:* The Independent, a bimonthly newsletter; National Directory of Computing and Consulting Services. *Student chapters:* no. *Recommended:* once you are a consultant, yes.

Institute for Certification of Computer Professionals (ICCP)

35 E. Wacker Drive
Chicago IL 60601
(312) 782-9437

Purpose: This organization was formed to provide certification programs aimed at standardizing an emerging computing profession. Two certificates are offered: Certificate in Data Processing and Certificate in Computer Programming. Other new certifications are currently being explored. Most industries have some form of credentializing, to have a standard from which others are judged. Being certified is one valuable part of your career. *Recommended:* highly, once you have been employed for several years.

International Information/Word Processing Association (IWP)

1015 North York Road
Willow Grove PA 19090
(215) 657-6300

Purpose: This organization gathers and disseminates information while acting as a clearinghouse for ideas about information and word processing. *Membership:* over 13,500 supervisory and management personnel actively engaged in information/word processing management, education, consulting, or marketing. *Events sponsored:* annual conference "Syntopican," symposium, executive briefings. *Publications:* Words, a bimonthly journal, technical newsletter, monographs, salary survey results, and more. *Recommended:* for supervisors and managers.

National Association of Computer Stores (NACS)

3255 South U.S. 1
Ft. Pierce FL 33450
(305) 465-9450

Purpose: This organization functions as a clearinghouse and representation arm for retailers of computers, in an effort to promote and make retailers knowledgeable. *Membership:* primary members are retail stores selling computers, their owners and managers. *Events sponsored:* annual meeting. *Publications:* NACS Newsletter. *Recommended:* if you plan to pursue a career in computer retailing, by all means join NACS as an individual if possible.

National Center for Computer Crime Data (NCCCD)

2700 N. Cahuenga Blvd., Suite 2113
Los Angeles CA 90068
(213) 850-0509

Purpose: This organization is a multifaceted information clearinghouse designed to facilitate the prevention, detection, investigation, and prosecution of computer crime. The center has a variety of resources available including legal work products, legislation, case summaries, scholarly materials, index to current research, and a network of experts. *Publications:* many reports dealing with computer crime. *Student chapters:* no. *Recommended:* for someone interested in the security aspect of computing, yes.

Operations Research Society of America (ORSA)

428 East Preston Street
Baltimore MD 21202
(301) 528-4146

Purpose: This organization advances the area of operations research through the exchange of information, establishment and maintenance of professional standards, and the encouragement of students of operations research. *Membership:* four types are available: full, associate, retired, and student; there are over 6,700 members. *Events sponsored:* joint national meetings with Institute of Management Sciences. *Publications:* Operations Research Journal, ORSA/TIMS Bulletin, Interfaces, OR/MS Today, and others. *Career information:* yes. *Student chapters:* about 10 student chapters across the country. *Recommended:* highly, once you choose a specialization in this area.

Optical Character Recognition (OCR) Users Association

P.O. Box 2016
Butterkill Arcade Bldg.
Manchester Center VT 05255

Purpose: This organization seeks to advance the techniques and applications of all recognition technologies as a means of capturing data. *Membership:* over 500 companies and individuals. *Events sponsored:* two conferences and exposition. *Publications:* bimonthly magazine—

OCR Today. *Student chapters:* no. *Recommended:* for those interested in optical character recognition, yes.

Society for Computer Medicine (SCM)

9650 Rockville Pike
Bethesda MD 20014
(301) 530-7120

Purpose: The major emphasis of the SCM is to provide and directly foster medical computing and make available a forum for understanding and continuing education in this new and emerging field. *Membership:* over 400 regular members and students. *Events sponsored:* annual meeting, computer medicine clinics/workshops. *Publications:* quarterly newsletter, annual meeting proceedings. *Student chapters:* no. *Recommended:* yes, if your interest lies in medical computing.

Society for Computer Simulation (SCS)

P.O. Box 2228
La Jolla CA 92038
(714) 459-3888

Purpose: This organization provides a forum for the interchange of ideas and dissemination of information on the art and science of computer simulation and modeling. *Membership:* over 3,300 members including regular, associate, senior, and students ($15.00). *Events sponsored:* regional simulation council meetings, technical committees. *Publications:* monthly magazine Simulation, semiannual proceedings. *Career information:* yes. *Student chapters:* yes. *Recommended:* yes.

Society for Information Display (SID)

654 North Sepulveda Blvd.
Los Angeles CA 90049
(213) 472-3550

Purpose: This organization promotes the advancement of information display through exchange of ideas and dissemination of information to its members. *Membership:* over 2,000; member ($15.00) and student ($3.00) available. *Events sponsored:* annual technical symposium, local chapters, field trips, tutorials. *Publications:* proceedings, bimonthly SID Journal, annual digest. *Recommended:* yes, after deciding on a specialty in this area.

Organizations

Society for Management Information Systems (SMIS)

111 E. Wacker Dr., Suite 600
Chicago IL 60601
(312) 644-6610

Purpose: To promote the effective use and judicious application of information resources toward solving management problems in both the private and public sectors. *Membership:* over 1,500 members; individual, academic, and student available. *Events sponsored:* annual conference, workshop, local chapters. *Publications:* MIS Journal, special publications. *Student chapters:* no. *Recommended:* yes, after you are in the field and progressing toward management positions.

Women in Information Processing (WIP)

1000 Connecticut Ave., N.W., Suite 9
Washington DC 20036
(202) 298-8000

Purpose: This is an international professional organization for career women in the computer, office-of-the-future, telecommunications, and related fields. Their goals are to expand career opportunities and provide a career structure and support network. *Membership:* over 3,200 women; regular ($40.00) and student ($25.00) available. *Events sponsored:* low-cost seminars, network meetings. *Publications:* PARITY Magazine. *Career information:* yes, WIP is heavily career oriented. *Recommended:* highly.

About the Author

Irv Brechner is President of Advantage Advertising Inc., an ad agency specializing in the microcomputer field. In addition, he publishes the InfoBook, a direct mail promotion for personal computer owners, and sells mailing lists, the AdPlanner and other projects in the same area.

He is the author of *The College Survival Kit,* a 250,000-copy best seller on making the adjustment to college, *The Career Finder,* recently introduced by Ballantine Books, and three introductory computer books, also recently released.

Mr. Brechner is married and lives in New Jersey.

36
4
20
-
87
20 -18 02
19

8790

38-51-11